The Tradition of Natural Taoism

"This is a wonderful summation of Taoist philosophy. Jason Gregory presents this cosmology clearly, concisely, and with great depth of understanding. If you want to gain a fuller understanding of commonly used terms such as the void, yin and yang, and nonduality, this book is for you."

SUSAN CAMPBELL, PH.D., AUTHOR OF
GETTING REAL AND *FROM TRIGGERED TO TRANQUIL*

"In this profound work, Jason Gregory warns us about the mass trivialization of Taoism. This book gives deep clarity to those who are called to flow effortlessly in the primordial river of Tao but find themselves perpetually obstructed by their deeply rooted habits of self-preservation. The time-honored virtues of humility, simplicity, and non-striving are elucidated brilliantly by the author, who offers the modern mind a possibility of venturing on the path of non-becoming. In our increasingly social world, the naked simplicity of The Way is not easy to follow, and this book is the much-needed guide that bridges this gap of understanding and allows the reader to embrace the natural naturalness that is Tao."

SWAMI ATMANANDA UDASIN, ADVAITA TEACHER AND
HEAD MONK OF AJATANANDA ASHRAM, RISHIKESH (INDIA)

"This book is an astonishing piece of work and one that is essential for anybody wishing a deeper understanding of not just Taoism but also Eastern philosophy in general. It introduces the reader to the explanatory power of this most fascinating of belief systems and places it within a precise context. It demands concentration and focus from the reader, but in doing so it gives great rewards. An absolutely essential read, and one destined to become a classic of its kind."

ANTHONY PEAKE, AUTHOR OF
OPENING THE DOORS OF PERCEPTION

"An interestingly complex yet simple book. It invites you to use your left brain for meaning and structure and your right brain, heart, and body to recognize the simple truths you see all around you in nature—and align with them for greater harmony—without great willpower or effort. It is certainly time we make life less confusing and distracting and settle into the calm center that we can recognize as Self, Truth, and Compassion. Jason has written many clarifying and inspiring books, and this one is a real wakeup call!"

PENNEY PEIRCE, AUTHOR OF *TRANSPARENCY*,
LEAP OF PERCEPTION, AND *FREQUENCY*

"Even though it is said that 'the Tao that can be spoken is not the true Tao,' Jason Gregory's words on Taoism lead us back to a felt awakening of our true nature. We are the Tao we seek, the flowing reality of our body's life. We just need to pare away what keeps us from connecting so deeply with the felt river of life that's here all the time. *The Tradition of Natural Taoism* shows us how to let go of what is superficial so we can engage once again with that which we are and always have been."

WILL JOHNSON, AUTHOR OF
THE RADICAL PATH OF SOMATIC DHARMA
AND *BREATHING THROUGH THE WHOLE BODY*

"This book provides the reader with a different perspective and a deeper understanding of the Tao (Dao) and Taoist texts. If you are interested in Tao, it is a profound reference book for your study."

YANG JWING-MING, AUTHOR OF
THE ROOT OF CHINESE QIGONG AND *THE DAO DE JING*

The Tradition of Natural Taoism

The Way of Free and Easy Wandering in Oneness

Jason Gregory

Inner Traditions
Rochester, Vermont

Inner Traditions
One Park Street
Rochester, Vermont 05767
www.InnerTraditions.com

Cataloging-in-Publication Data for this title is available from the Library of Congress

ISBN 979-8-88850-235-8 (print)
ISBN 979-8-88850-236-5 (ebook)

Printed and bound in the United States by Lake Book Manufacturing, LLC

10 9 8 7 6 5 4 3 2 1

Text design by Kira Kariakin and layout by Kenleigh Manseau
This book was typeset in Garamond Premier Pro with Manofa and Raleway used as display typefaces.

To send correspondence to the author of this book, mail a first-class letter to the author c/o Inner Traditions, One Park Street, Rochester, VT 05767, and we will forward the communication, or contact the author directly at **jasongregory.org**.

Scan the QR code and save 25% at InnerTraditions.com. Browse over 2,000 titles on spirituality, the occult, ancient mysteries, new science, holistic health, and natural medicine.

Dedicated to the ancient Taoist masters
Lao-tzu and Chuang-tzu.
May their truth of oneness continue
to enlighten the world.

Contents

Acknowledgments ix

INTRODUCTION Reclaiming Taoism 1

1 The Human Reflection of the Universe 14

2 Taoism's Critique of
Confucianism and Socialization 43

3 The Dissolution of Identity 63

4 The Immorality of Morality 85

5 Beyond Good and Evil 109

6 The Simple World vs. the Complex World 132

7 The Art of Doing Nothing 149

8 The Spontaneous Reality 165

9 Free and Easy Wandering in Oneness 180

Notes 194

Bibliography 198

Index 204

Acknowledgments

The Tradition of Natural Taoism: The Way of Free and Easy Wandering in Oneness is the result of a sustained contemplation on the tradition of Taoism, stretching for more than two decades. What I knew about Taoism as a wee grasshopper is minuscule compared to what I know now due to my continual travels around the world meeting scholars, philosophers, and teachers, alongside my own private study and practice. Like anyone who first comes across Taoism, I, too, was a young person who thought I had a good understanding because the most available literature on Taoism is often watered down and, from a nontraditional perspective, infused with a Western perspective. I am extremely thankful I came across the right knowledge and people at the right time who steered me in the right direction, which has helped me teach Taoism as it is, rather than how many people want it to be or how my younger self naively believed it to be. To all of those masters, students, friends, and supposed foes who have enriched my own personal journey and understanding, thank you.

The bulk of this book was written in Brisbane when I returned to my home state of Queensland in Australia and basically locked myself in a small apartment for six months to give my undivided attention to reviving and hopefully restoring the tradition of Taoism to its rightful place. Alongside Brisbane, I had the pleasure of editing and adding parts of the book in Chiang Mai, Thailand, a magical place where I have written many of my previous books. To all of the amazing people of Brisbane and Chiang Mai, thank you for providing an atmosphere conducive to deep contemplation.

Everything I have achieved as an author is not possible without my wife, Gayoung. You are the spiritual backbone of my life that keeps me centered and focused on what truly matters. The life we've built together dedicated to the truth is something I thought, once upon a time, was inconceivable. Our lives continue to unfold in a beautiful way where every day is as joyful as the next. As a result, we are privileged to experience the true joy of life, not only together but also with others in person and from afar who have been touched in the heart by my books and YouTube channel and our podcast together. When I think of my love for you and our life together, I am reminded of the Sanskrit phrase *Om Paramar Mainamar*, which means our union is dedicated to the Ultimate. I love you.

For over a decade, I have had the good fortune to be published by Inner Traditions. But being published by Inner Traditions was not possible without acquisitions editor Jon Graham believing in my work. There are no words that would be sufficient to extend my heartfelt gratitude to you, Jon. Your support and belief in my work are things I don't take for granted. You are always honest with me and know when to push me to get the most out of my books. I am blessed to have your ongoing support and also to have worked with you closely over the years.

Next, I owe a special debt of gratitude to the two editors of this book. First, a big thank you to my copy editor Ceylan Ozguner. Your gratitude and positive reflections on my book during the editing process were very refreshing. I'm just grateful you enjoyed my book as much as I enjoyed hearing your support for it. Secondly, I want to share my heartfelt gratitude to my project editor Meghan

MacLean. This is the sixth book we've worked on together, and I wouldn't have wanted to do it with anyone else. You are always so meticulous during the editing process and know how to make my work shine. The holistic overview you have for editing is directly reflected in this book. I deeply appreciate the time and care you've shown my work over the years.

The majority of my books would not have had life breathed into them without the heart and soul of Inner Traditions, Ehud Sperling. It is with humble gratitude that I thank you for believing in my work. In an age when some publishers are selling out to illogical popular narratives for the corporate dollar, you have kept the integrity of Inner Traditions alive and well, where the reader can trust that your original intent back in its founding year of 1975 is the same in the present. You should feel proud that Inner Traditions is a beacon of spiritual light for the world.

Last but definitely not least, it is with the utmost respect that I thank the two great ancient sages of Taoism, Lao-tzu and Chuang-tzu. There is no Taoism without either, and if it weren't for the Tao Te Ching and Chuang-tzu texts, then the authentic way of nature would have been lost to a world yearning for control. I am eternally grateful that as a young person, I never stopped my curiosity and inquiry into the nature of the Tao, and instead I doubled down on absorbing my mind and heart into the tradition both these sages left behind for all of us to learn and become wiser. I hope that *The Tradition of Natural Taoism* carries both of their wisdom forth into the distant future and beyond.

Note on the Romanization of Chinese Words

There are two commonly known Romanization systems for Chinese words. The older and more familiar one is known as the Wade-Giles, while the new standard and more precise one is the Pinyin Romanization. For example, the Chinese word 道 in the Wade-Giles system is *Tao*, and this is the Romanization with which many people are familiar. It is somewhat pleasing aesthetically but its sound is not quite accurate. On the other hand, the Pinyin Romanization of this word is *Dao*. Many are not familiar with this spelling, nor, we may say, is it as aesthetically pleasing, but its sound is more accurate.

In this book, I have blended both systems of Romanization for Chinese and given the spelling of both when we are first introduced to a significant Chinese word that will be a core Taoist principle to remember throughout the book. The Romanization I choose for each Chinese word throughout is based on what I believe people are most familiar with and also what I feel is best aesthetically.

Reclaiming Taoism

Taoism (道教: Wade-Giles *Taoism*; Pinyin *Daoism*) is essentially a philosophy based on the way of nature. But even that statement on its own can be misinterpreted due to one's own personal, social, cultural, or religious understanding of the way of nature. For Taoism, even though this definition seems self-explanatory, it is complex to understand and even more difficult to live by. This entire book will explain what it truly means to be in accord with and to follow the way of nature, the Tao (道: Wade-Giles *Tao*; Pinyin *Dao*). But before that, we truly need to comprehend that Taoism is essentially a natural philosophy.

In the age of information saturation, Taoism, like much else, has fallen victim to misunderstanding, misinterpretation, and misinformation. Its nature is essentially mysterious, so if one has not studied Taoist philosophy extensively, a warped view of the tradition eventuates that, unfortunately, influences other people not schooled in Taoism. It is a constant cycle of misinformation, which has been ramped up since the advent and increased popularity of social media platforms such as YouTube.

These platforms perpetuate misinformation about Taoism, especially that based on incorrect translations of the Tao Te Ching (道德經: Wade-Giles *Tao Te Ching*; Pinyin *Daodejing*) and

Chuang-tzu (莊子: Wade-Giles *Chuang-tzu*; Pinyin *Zhuangzi*) texts. Unfortunately, a lot of these incorrect translations are the most popular versions of these texts—particularly of the Tao Te Ching. These versions have been stripped of their original meaning to make sense to a predominantly Western audience with certain cultural sensibilities. They are easier to follow and poetic for Western minds. Many people enjoy reading them because they relate to us in the here and now. Even I enjoy reading them occasionally. But at the end of the day, they are not correct and distort the original meaning and intent of the Taoist texts.

The most accurate translations are vague and mysterious to the untrained mind. They require deeper contemplation and understanding. They require us to understand the real nuanced meaning of each line from what was truly written in Chinese. Each chapter and rereading elicit a new layer of understanding. We cannot honestly come to a conclusion on those texts after one reading. A deeper inquiry is needed. One that cannot happen in short spurts like five-to-ten-minute YouTube videos based on unclear translations. If you are serious about Taoism, then it is imperative to understand its genuine essence and what it truly is.

A NEED FOR STRUCTURE

Though it may seem counterintuitive to the way of Taoism, there is a growing need for structure and clarity on what Taoism is and, essentially, what it means to be Taoist. Despite the lucid, effortless nature of Taoism, we live in an age where some framework is needed to avoid a complete disfiguration of the tradition. It is not just about knowing what particular aspects of Taoism are or even experiencing them, but rather a complete understanding of the tradition is required that will transform your psychology and worldview.

Based on the way of the Tao, many different systems of cultivation were created over the thousands of years since the time of the great Taoist sages Lao-tzu (老子: Wade-Giles *Lao-tzu*; Pinyin *Laozi*) and Chuang-tzu (369–286 BCE) in China's Warring States period. Most notable are the cultivation methods of martial arts and Traditional Chinese Medicine (TCM) based on the holistic philosophy of Taoism. More precisely, these two branches are known in Chinese as *Neidan*, internal alchemy, and *Waidan*, external alchemy. The internal alchemy of Neidan is cultivated through the well-known martial and nonmartial arts spiritual practices of *t'ai chi ch'uan* (commonly known as t'ai chi), *qi gong, baguazhang, xingyiquan, liuhebafa,* and *daoyin*, which are all part of what is known as *Nei Gong*. The external alchemy of Waidan is practiced through herbal elixirs, specific foods, and other physiological practices all related to a holistic view of the human body and mind. Both Neidan and Waidan are based on the tenets of holism, which is the essence of Taoism, and a fundamental understanding of oneness that we will explore throughout this book.

Such traditions and lineages stemming from Taoist philosophy have developed and been refined for thousands of years. Personally, I am actively engaged in both Neidan and Waidan, and I can tell you from experience that if both are informed by their original philosophy of Taoism, then they will transform your life. A common misconception people have is if they practice t'ai chi ch'uan, for example, this makes them a Taoist. Nothing could be further from the truth. That would be like saying anyone who practices hatha yoga is a Hindu. Hatha yoga is a small part of Hinduism, but you don't have to practice hatha yoga to be Hindu. Likewise, you don't have to practice t'ai chi ch'uan, qi gong, or Waidan to be Taoist. Will they deepen your understanding and experience of Tao? Yes, of course, especially if they are informed by Taoist philosophy. But are they necessary to follow the Tao? No.

Taoism is essentially an attitude, behavior, and worldview shaped by nature and not human socialization. Some people have an inherent aptitude for Taoism, and others need cultivation. Both depend on various factors: your genetic blueprint, your past life karma, your upbringing, culture, and religious indoctrination. Nevertheless, the Tao is ever-present, *immanent within all experience*, and at the same time *transcends all experience*. There is no one way to align yourself with the irreducible essence of Tao, though we could say Neidan, meditation practices, simplifying your life, and other practices are all effective methods. But, keep in mind, if you don't understand the philosophy of Taoism, then no matter how much you practice meditation, for example, the experience and depth of the Tao within your being will not be realized.

Taoism requires a complete transformation via a dedication to unlearning the socialization we've all endured, which is not an easy feat. Taoism is a technology for deprogramming our minds from socialization so that we can finally return to our original natural state. Returning to our basic disposition can, ironically, be one of the hardest things we can do, as physicist Fritjof Capra explains when describing Zen in relation to our innate naturalness:

> The perfection of Zen is thus to live one's everyday life naturally and spontaneously. When Po-chang was asked to define Zen, he said, "When hungry eat, when tired sleep." Although this sounds simple and obvious, like so much in Zen, it is in fact quite a difficult task. To regain the naturalness of our original nature requires long training and constitutes a great spiritual achievement.[1]

Taoism, like Zen, is a philosophy that guides us back to our true, original nature. As Capra mentioned, regaining this naturalness is more difficult than it seems. This is made even more difficult in the modern world because people are influenced by incorrect translations and cultural biases that we project onto Taoism like everything else. This leads to *radical universalism*, where Taoism is undermined by other cultures, especially Western cultures, with differing religions and social beliefs. Sure, it is true that Taoism adapts to anyone of any faith or disposition because when you understand the Tao, you realize that it encompasses all (even your God). But the main problem is that Taoism is treated as a secondary philosophy one applies to their religion, culture, or social disposition. For example, you can be Christian and follow the Tao because it encompasses all, every single part of your life. However, in its truest context, you can't be a Christian and *really* follow the Tao because they are philosophically different. Someone could say they are Christian but abide by the philosophy and principles of Taoism, but that in fact makes them Taoist, not Christian. They are essentially Lao-tzu in Christian disguise.

THE DANGERS OF CULTURAL APPROPRIATION

To honestly understand Taoism, or to be Taoist, requires one to follow the way of nature, which actually runs counter to many other religions and social beliefs. Hence the need for structure and understanding of true Taoism to avoid such cultural appropriation. And I know the clear rebuttal to this idea is that Taoism is a path that has no solidity, no dogma, and this is what makes it so successful. This is true, and I don't disagree. But to avoid ongoing cultural and traditional appropriation of Taoism, we need to have a thorough understanding of the philosophy without any additional beliefs that run counter to Taoism, stopping us from walking the spiritual path unfettered.

One of the primary states of consciousness in Taoism is Chuang-tzu's *free and easy wandering*, which I will speak about at length in the last chapter of this book. If there is a blockage in our way from the natural experience of free and easy wandering, then that ought to be reevaluated under the microscope of Taoist philosophy. If we don't have this mentality and our worldview is different from Taoism, then this is where the teachings slowly get warped over time until eventually the original teachings become devoid of meaning.

Taoist practitioner and independent scholar Eva Wong warned us about this cultural and traditional appropriation coming especially from the West in the 1990s. Wong used the Richard Wilhelm translation of the I Ching to illustrate her point of this distorting of Taoist knowledge. The Wilhelm translation comes with an amazing foreword by famous psychiatrist and psychoanalyst Carl Jung. I've read this version many times, and I do enjoy it. But what a young me didn't know at the time was that this version of the I Ching is influenced by a tinge of Western thought. Wong revealed that the Wilhelm translation is, in part, seen through the lens of Jungian psychology, a Western viewpoint. How much so is debatable. But her point is that the translation of the I Ching is not interpreted from the Taoist view, nor is it put in its historical context. This acknowledgment of the lens and historical context of a translation is a point we must always consider when we read translations of any ancient text. To honestly translate the I Ching, it must be understood from its historical and philosophical context and not through the prism of another school of thought, such as Jungian psychology. Just this one revelation by Eva Wong has inspired me to explore other translations of the I Ching in the past decade. I am grateful I did. If we understand Taoism from its historical context, then its philosophy will shine forth because we understand what circumstances gave birth to it—the minds of the original Taoists. Taoism must be understood as it is with no filters.

We must have no cultural bias when learning a new tradition

and enter into the endeavor with a completely open mind. And yes, that will be difficult, but that is what is needed to completely assimilate a new (or in Taoism's case, the original) worldview. And so to be a genuine Taoist, you don't see the world through your psychological and societal conditioning, but rather from the way of the ancients—more precisely from the way of Lao-tzu and Chuang-tzu.

THE ROOT OF TAOISM

Even though t'ai chi ch'uan, qi gong, and TCM have become synonymous with Taoism, they are only a few branches produced by the original root. When we think of the root of Taoism, we must only think of the great sages Lao-tzu and Chuang-tzu. There are other Taoist sages who came centuries later, and their teachings are based on the teachings of Lao-tzu and Chuang-tzu, too, such as Lieh-tzu and Wen-tzu. Their teachings are important, but it's necessary to understand the depth of the teachings of Lao-tzu and Chuang-tzu first.

Make no mistake about it, Taoism is based on the texts of the Tao Te Ching and Chuang-tzu, attributed to Lao-tzu and Chuang-tzu respectively. If you want to be a Taoist, then you need to study and contemplate both texts thoroughly. In the fifteen-plus years I've been teaching Eastern philosophy, I am astounded by the number of times I converse with martial arts students who don't study either text. Some of them don't even know about them at all, nor do they know Lao-tzu and Chuang-tzu. Once someone asked me if the Tao Te Ching was related to Taoism, which is just plain odd considering the Tao Te Ching *is* Taoism and its actual root. This strange comment highlights the danger of the great tradition of Taoism being used as a commodity. It may seem sometimes as though nothing is sacred anymore in the twenty-first century, but these ancient traditions are naturally sacred and deserve our respect.

The problem with studying Taoism is you need to be skilled at discernment when searching for information. You don't want to be led down the garden path of misinformation. To avoid that is simple; find genuine translations of the Tao Te Ching and Chuang-tzu texts, and allow your mind to be absorbed in the way of nature. Lao-tzu and Chuang-tzu will guide you there. They will reveal the Tao as the ever-present force moving through you *as* you.

Historically, Lao-tzu and Chuang-tzu were radical sages in the Warring States period of China, a time heavily dominated by Confucianism (儒家: Wade-Giles *Ju-chia*; Pinyin *Rujia*). Ironically, nothing has changed. The ideologies, the governments, the religions, and the cultures are different, but still being a Taoist is radically different from the status quo. Being genuinely as nature is and following its way runs counter to human socialization. That is a big takeaway you'll gain from this book. But it is nothing new for Taoists. Every Taoist since the time of those sages has had to live in a world so far disconnected from the source, and this distance is constantly growing generation after generation due to the gravitational pull of the external world and materialism.

Lao-tzu and Chuang-tzu ran counter to this type of socialization in a Confucian world, and so should we in the present day because socialization itself is a superimposition on our true nature, making us feel artificial and like a cheap replica of the original (I will explore this superimposition later in the book).

Being a true Taoist, then, means to be radically rebellious, not in an anarchistic or self-righteous way, but instead because you're indifferent to the world. What motivates most people is none of your concern. Your center is the Tao, and this is what informs your life, not what is trending. Taoism will liberate you from the shackles and suffering that are both intrinsic to the nature of a society built on man-made ideologies and materialism. This is the gift Lao-tzu and Chuang-tzu gave us. Their call to us is to ask, "How radical are we willing to be?" To follow the way of the Tao runs counter to conventional thinking, but it is the way the world sincerely is at its core.

TAOISM MUST MIGRATE FROM CHINA TO SURVIVE

For any of this to happen, Taoism needs to transcend the border of China. Sure, the birth of Taoism is from China through the great sages Lao-tzu and Chuang-tzu, but for its survival it is imperative it migrates to other lands in its pure form. One reason for this necessity is the slow destruction of Taoism, and also Buddhism, since the Cultural Revolution in China. Even in the present day, Communist China is hell-bent on destroying alternative ideologies, and freedom of religion is under attack.

I have a lot of Chinese friends and have had interviews with popular newspapers in China, and, astonishingly, many of them know little about Taoism and know more about Marxism instead. This is not to say that Taoism is not still alive in China. It is alive and, in some places, thriving. The restoration of Taoism in China is important, but it will take some time, depending on people losing faith in the totalitarianism of Marxism or communism. But unfortunately, in China, there's the same misapprehension as in the West that practicing t'ai chi ch'uan, for example, makes you Taoist. Lao-tzu and Chuang-tzu's philosophy becomes background noise to spiritual practices and postures. Again, the philosophy must inform the practices, not the other way around.

One of the most common mistakes I encounter is how to follow *wu-wei* (無為: Wade-Giles *wu-wei*; Pinyin *wu-wei*), which is translated as "effortless action," "effortless living," "nondoing," "intelligent spontaneity," or "non-interference." People all over the world want to apply wu-wei to their extremely busy and complex lives. But they make no effort to simplify their lives. Without simplicity, the possibility of being in wu-wei is very low, considering simplicity is the fertile soil for the growth of an effortless mind. When it comes to wu-wei, people in general overthink and are truthfully not ready to allow life to be as it will with no interference. We often live super complex lives within very complex societies, making it even more difficult for wu-wei to eventuate. This complexity is rife in many countries in both the West and the East, places where people have little time outside their subservience to the machinations of society. In Far East Asia, including China, South Korea, and Japan, it is extremely difficult to keep up with what is expected, as these countries have gone far from their roots of simplicity.

Taoism will survive in China, but the danger is it might be isolated to the hermits in the mountains. Likewise, if real Taoism doesn't spread beyond China, then the tradition may survive only through a few weirdos like myself and other teachers outside of China. This type of threat has always existed for Taoism, even when it was first developed. The reason being that Taoism has never been widely accepted nor its philosophy lived by more than a few oddballs (likely you reading this book).

Often standing in the way of Taoism are social systems of control that belittle such a tradition because, from the status quo's perspective, how could a society be governed through no control? This fear not only pervades a social system but also the individual. For this reason, Taoism has never been taken seriously or followed truthfully on a large scale. Ironically, Taoism is the way of nature, yet we are under the belief that our human desire for control and social structures supersede nature. Oh, how we are wrong.

TIME TO ACCEPT TAOISM AS IT IS

Taoism has never been widely accepted because we lack the ability to be radically human, flaws and all. We are constantly at odds with our own humanity. Just being a natural human is a challenge for many of us because we've all been put through the wringer of socialization, which warps our original nature. Our parents tell us to succeed, education tells us what is useful for society, religion teaches us that we need to find God to be saved, and all of it, every little bit, is based on our ignorance and avoidance of our true nature.

Many religions, for example, will create all sorts of assumptions about life after death to try and alleviate our fear of death. They essentially use fear to intimidate people to implement systems of discipline the religion recommends. They prey on all our natural anxieties, not just the ones we have of death. Taoism, on the other hand, subverts belief systems that cultivate a fear of death to control people's behavior and emotions. Taoism wants you to explore those anxieties we have for such mysteries so that we free ourselves from the worries of death by understanding the fact that we neither know the transformations that preceded our existence nor those to come. Taoism asks you to lean into the uncertainties involved in being human.

We learn to be indifferent to death through Taoism. From Chuang-tzu's perspective, who is to say death is a terrible or joyful experience? (Chuang-tzu is not referring to the duration of dying, but just death itself.) We are only making fearful assumptions based on the affirmation of life. Well, Taoism takes it a step further and is a tradition centered on the affirmation of life and also death. Death is natural to life and something that we shouldn't be anxious about. When we are at odds with our own humanity, then things such as death are confusing and something we do our best to avoid.

Taoism welcomes natural transformations. Experiencing the natural transformations of life is just what humans do. We shouldn't fight this reality but instead embrace it. Embracing our humanity, flaws and all, is the massive difference between Taoism and many other religions. Taoism has no doctrine to impose on you; rather it is a technology to deprogram all of the indoctrination you've experienced, to give you a thorough understanding of your true nature. Instead of fighting your natural inclinations, Taoism wants you to explore them and inquire into their nature to see if they are pure or not.

Many religions teach us to fight our natural instincts and intuitions under the impression that humans are uncultured beasts. Taoism, on the other hand, teaches us to embrace our nature and understand that any self-cultivation method is actually what can turn us into beasts (something I will explore more in chapter two). Most of us have rarely or never been taught to accept ourselves as we are. In a roundabout way, society, some religions, education, and, in some cases, our friends and family subtly cultivate in us a sense of not being good enough as we are and also that we don't belong. Taoism's the opposite. It explains that we are innately good enough and that we do belong. We actually cannot be disowned. This natural belonging and intrinsic value are big factors as to why it is hard for someone to truthfully follow the Tao when they are part of a different religious or philosophical worldview.

We are so shortsighted when we try to discredit Taoism. We will make up all sorts of excuses why Taoism doesn't work: How can we be fundamentally good when we see the bad actions of others? How can allowing nature to run its course without interference achieve anything? We can't see that, for example, it is society that creates people with wrong intentions, and so it should be the social structures and belief systems that should be reevaluated. We have built the world in reverse, where the world is informing you rather than you informing the world. The Tao is not induced in us but rather moves through us naturally. Nature is grown from within to without to beautify the world. But if the conditions are wrong and we accept this reverse system of without to within, then this is where all sorts of trouble begins. The reverse stream is basically the template for many differing schools of thought—the idea that Tao is induced rather than naturally within us. Taoism is the way of radically reversing this stream to its original position.

Instead of criticizing Taoism from fear of it being so different, why not just try it and test it for yourself? It is hard to honestly criticize something unless you've been intimate with it. The irony is, when we criticize Taoism, we are criticizing ourselves and nature, which is in part why we have a domineering relationship to nature. The fundamental point is most of us have never tried Taoism wholeheartedly. We've rarely given it a chance outside of how it will benefit us and accentuate our preexisting beliefs. We have almost never been taught to accept ourselves the way we are as humans. We've almost always been uncomfortable in our own skin, so we designed all sorts of beliefs to make sense of life and alleviate this unnecessary discomfort. But what is staring us in our faces all the time is that we need to accept the human condition rather than avoid it.

In avoiding the human condition, we suppress our nature, which causes all sorts of psychological damage and social unrest. It is through accepting the human condition that equanimity of mind and peace on Earth will prevail. Taoism, the way of nature, is that vehicle waiting for all of us if we are willing to accept it wholeheartedly.

Taoism is pushing humanity to evolve by being radically human, not some transcendent philosophy about overcoming our humanity. We need to lean into our humanity to push through the boundaries that divide us from each other and the Tao. It's about understanding your true nature as it is with no filters. This very book is an attempt to revive the actual teachings of Taoism as they are. In the end, this book is about the true way of nature, your actual nature, because, well, that's the way it is.

1
The Human Reflection of the Universe

The fundamental belief in the world is that we are separate from everything. Even in many religions, we are separate from God, which is actually a perspective of this fundamental belief in separation. Taoism, on the other hand, runs counter to this belief for good reason. In Taoism, the big picture and the small picture are the *same* picture. The microcosm is the macrocosm and vice versa. There is no separation or distance between the source of the Tao and the source of your very being.

The ultimate reality of the Tao and your own localization of consciousness are the same, just different vantage points of the same reality. You essentially are a reflection of the entire universe. All of the fundamental forces of the universe move through us *as* us, but we confuse this experience with subjectivity, which essentially separates us from the source, the Tao. However, keep in mind that you can never be separate from the Tao; that is just an illusion of the subjective self, ego, and identity that is under the hypnosis that it is isolated from everyone and everything. Our ego, then, serves as a blockage to the fundamental forces of the universe moving through us.

Since the origin of the universe, the birth of the *ten thousand things* in Taoist terminology or the big bang in scientific terminology, those elemental forces are still moving through the universe and through our very being. These fundamental forces are ever-present, and we can align with them and utilize them when we have removed the blockage of self, ego, or identity. We are an aperture for the Tao to express itself, but none of that can eventuate when we are holding on to our separate sense of self (more on this later in the book).

The Tao is that ultimate reality that is all and everything, and we can sense it in our lives when we have taken the humble low path of Lao-tzu and Chuang-tzu. The Tao cannot be felt through a form of over-the-top strict cultivation or striving, but rather in letting go of yourself and the negative tendency to control your life and the world. From the place of your original existence and nature, you are a perfect reflection of the entire universe. What eclipses this is the accumulative sense of self we become due to socialization from society throughout our lives. For this reason, Lao-tzu's Tao Te Ching deals with our permanent original nature so that we can be our authentic selves. As philosopher Jacob Needleman explained:

The *Tao Te Ching* deals with what is permanent in us. It speaks of a possible inner greatness and an equally possible inner failure, which are both indelibly written into our very structure as human beings. Under its gaze, we are not "American" or "Chinese" or "European." We are human beings, uniquely called to occupy a specific place in the cosmic order, no matter where or in what era we live.

The *Tao Te Ching* is thus a work of metaphysical psychology, taking us far beyond the social or biological factors that have been the main concern of modern psychology. It helps us see how the fundamental forces of the cosmos itself are mirrored in our own individual, inner structure. And it invites us to try to live in direct relationship to all these forces. To see truly and to live fully: This is what it means to be authentically human.[1]

That eternal original nature within us is the position the authentic person resides in—the consciousness of a Taoist sage. The sage has reversed their trajectory from separation (the ten thousand things) to the Tao (nondual oneness). This reversal of one's trajectory is a perceptual shift, where our awareness has moved from the external world to the internal world, which is how we align with the fundamental forces of the universe, the Tao. To attain the same consciousness as a Taoist sage is not easy; it requires a complete reorientation of thinking and perceiving the world, which have both, unfortunately, been hijacked by the fundamental belief in separation through duality and the gravitational pull of the material world. Thankfully, the Taoist sages of ancient times left a spiritual road map for us to follow so that we can return to our nature to finally realize that the Tao is doing you instead of you are doing the Tao.

THE METAPHYSICAL COSMOLOGY OF TAO

The metaphysical cosmology of the Tao is reflected in the very nature of our being. It is not only a scientific view of the universe but also an understanding of how the small picture of a human being is a reflection of the big picture of the whole, the Tao. This knowledge existed in differing form pre-Taoism but gained a deeper understanding from early Taoism to present day.

In both pre- and early Taoism they discovered three key concepts to understanding the unfolding of the Tao as the universe and how that is reflected in our nature. These three concepts are *wu chi* (無極: Wade-Giles *wu chi*; Pinyin *wuji*), *t'ai chi* (太極: Wade-Giles *t'ai chi*;

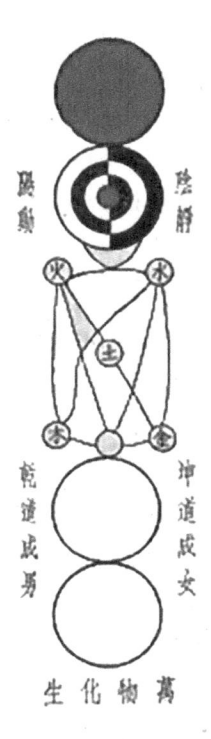

Ming-era Taoist T'ai chi t'u

Pinyin *taiji*), and yin yang (陰陽: Wade-Giles *yin yang*; Pinyin *yin yang*), which I'll explain in the next sections. These three concepts are familiar to martial arts practitioners in a practical application. All three are represented in one of the traditional Taoist diagrams of the T'ai chi t'u (太極圖: Wade-Giles *T'ai chi t'u*; Pinyin *Taijitu*), which is a symbol or diagram representing the supreme ultimate of Tao from the Ming era (1368–1644 CE).

The T'ai chi t'u consists of five parts, including wu chi, t'ai chi, and yin yang. At the top of the diagram is an empty circle depicting the absolute, wu chi. The second circle represents t'ai chi and the natural, mutual opposition of yin yang. Below the second circle is the five-part diagram of the Chinese Five Elements or Phases known in Chinese as *wuxing* (五行: Wade-Giles *wu-hsing*; Pinyin *wuxing*), which represents a further movement from oneness to multiplicity. The circle below the Chinese Five Elements represents the conjunction of Heaven and Earth, which gives rise to the ten thousand things (the dualistic manifest world). The final circle represents the ten thousand things in their final stage of multiplicity, the world we all know too well. I will explain the three foundational concepts of wu chi, t'ai chi, and yin yang that give birth to Heaven, Earth, and the ten thousand things. Many people are familiar with t'ai chi and yin yang, but not with wu chi, and that is where we ought to start.

Wu Chi

Wu chi is the unmanifested aspect of Tao. It is the infinite void of nothingness, which, in the T'ai chi t'u, is represented by the empty circle at the top of the diagram. Wu chi is the Tao in stillness, the undifferentiated timelessness before the origin of the universe. So before all sets of opposites were set in motion by the origin of the universe, there was wu chi. Wu chi, then, is the essential nondual nature of the universe. The nondual reality of wu chi illustrates how the inherent nature of the Tao is nothingness. Tao essentially is meontological; it is without qualities, which is exactly the same as *Nirguna Brahman* in Advaita Vedanta (Tao and Brahman are identical concepts). But in both the nothingness of Tao and Brahman, there is an intrinsic power that creates. In chapter five of the Tao Te Ching, Lao-tzu uses the bellows to illustrate this inherent power within nothingness:

> The space between heaven and earth
> is like a bellows.
> The shape changes but not the form;
> The more it moves, the more it yields.[2]

The nothingness of the bellows is wu chi, and in the bellows, as we see in the T'ai chi t'u, its nature is to create and move. This is similar to the wheel and hub description used in the Chuang-tzu text. The hub is infinitely empty, yet the spokes of the wheel depend on the hub for its motion. Chuang-tzu himself explained this state of wu chi consciousness in the Chuang-tzu text:

> *When there is no more separation between "this" and "that," it is called the still-point of the Tao. At the still-point in the center of the circle one can see the infinite in all things.*[3]

I will explain the dissolution of opposites that Chuang-tzu experienced in later chapters. The nothingness of wu chi embodies the power of Tao. We experience this personally when we consistently meditate deeply, which allows the stream of consciousness to flow through us without any ego blockage disturbing the stream. In doing so, the right course of action and our all-round intellectual life are allowed to grow and prosper through a tranquil mind. The more you meditate, the more you access this infinite well-spring. I've experienced this personally as a writer and video creator. The more we access the hub of wu chi, the more the wheel begins to turn in harmony with all things. Inherent within wu chi, as we see with the bellows and the hub, is a power of motion, a power of creation. This movement from nothing to everything is fundamental to the second and third key concepts of t'ai chi and yin and yang.

T'ai Chi and Yin Yang Theory

T'ai chi is very well-known around the world through the practice of t'ai chi ch'uan. But what is less well-known is the actual philosophy of t'ai chi, which a lot of Nei Gong practices, including t'ai chi

T'ai chi symbol of yin and yang

ch'uan, are built on. While wu chi is the Tao in stillness, t'ai chi, on the other hand, is the Tao in motion. It is the spark of power that emerges out of the nothingness of Tao (wu chi) to create the motion of energy at the foundation of the universe. T'ai chi is the oscillation and vibratory modulation that allows the defined form of manifestation to be born of the infinite nothingness of wu chi.

The movement of t'ai chi out of wu chi creates yin and yang. Actually, t'ai chi *is* yin and yang. The integration of yin and yang in the famous symbol is called t'ai chi, as this symbol encapsulates the entire energy and motion of the manifest world, the ten thousand things as Lao-tzu would say.

The movement of t'ai chi creates the two primary energies of the universe, yin and yang. Intrinsically within movement (t'ai chi) is yin and yang. The process of t'ai chi and yin and yang creates opposites, the duality we believe we experience subjectively. As the Tao Te Ching states:

> The Tao begot one.
> One begot two.
> Two begot three
> And three begot the ten thousand things.[4]

Yin means the feminine, receptive, physical, and Earth principle, while yang means the masculine, active, nonphysical, and heavenly principle. It's important not to confuse the feminine and masculine with man or woman. Yin and yang are energetic qualities every human possesses, no matter their gender. Also, do not confuse Taoist heavens with a Christian version of Heaven as a place someone goes after death. Heaven and Earth in the Taoist view are that which is above, the heavens (space), and that which is below, earth (solid ground/nature).

A human is a conduit between Heaven and Earth, a receptor of the fundamental forces of the universe in a bidirectional manner. Yin and yang are, then, the energetic building blocks of the manifest world set in motion by t'ai chi. For Heaven and Earth to be in rhythmic balance within the universe, yin and yang have to be in perfect harmony, and intrinsically they are macrocosmically. Microcosmically, on the other hand, is a different story. Yin and yang are often imbalanced in humans.

The perfect harmony of yin and yang is often thwarted due to our constant mental movement into the external world. Our pure awareness is entangled with the external world due to the motion (t'ai chi) of our awareness being trained in only one direction, out. When the t'ai chi movement of awareness is geared externally, this creates a separate and isolated ego. This external perception is the byproduct of the fundamental human belief in separation. We are all trained under the illusion of this belief in separation of the physical from the spiritual, in duality. As a result, as we grow in this life, we accumulate a sense of self that is not natural to us but rather is the creation of the external world and the socialization we go through by society and culture. The ego, or rather the self-identity, you think you are essentially is not you, and, in actuality, it belongs to the external world because it is the external world that created and defined it, for the most part.

Our perceptual trajectory of motion is geared in the wrong direction because of the belief in the duality of separation. Macrocosmically, t'ai chi moves out of wu chi and is in constant creational movement through the constituents of yin and yang. But none of this is possible without the internal power of Tao residing in the nothingness of wu chi. Universal harmony and evolution are possible only due to the t'ai chi motion being in perfect symmetry with wu chi. The problem is this motion from the source is mirrored in our perceptual faculties. Our pure awareness's trajectory, then, is mainly external. Taoist sages were acutely aware of this phenomenon. As a result, spiritual practices such as t'ai chi ch'uan and many other meditative practices were created to reverse the trajectory from the ten thousand things to wu chi so that we fully and completely reside and are aligned with the Tao.

THE MOTION OF RETURN

Skilled meditation practitioners for thousands of years have been a living example and evidence that the motion of t'ai chi is not one-directional. The great sages and spiritual masters have always stood as the spiritual guides back to Tao. But unfortunately, our society has been solely possessed for thousands of years on a one-directional external approach to motion. Hence, we've often lived in a confused world with confused people. The internal world is frequently overlooked and, in this day and age, almost forgotten completely by many.

The external trajectory of t'ai chi can only continue to solidify your ego identity. The solidity of identity, then, contributes to fragmentation within society because its basis is separation. Practically everyone is playing this game. Group ideologies and the overidentification with identity are all due to the hypnotic belief in separation. Our perception is continually oriented externally, and we read the environment as such for our own survival. We find safe haven within a group in which we believe we belong, but this act of security paradoxically creates division because to belong to one group pits one against another. So inherently within security is division and insecurity; as Jiddu Krishnamurti explained: "And we thought there was security in the family, security in the tribe, security in nationalism. So we thought there was security in division. The very division creates insecurity."[5]

Such hypnosis is only possible with an externally geared view of reality. But, as I've said, the motion of Tao (t'ai chi) is not one-directional. Actually, to know our source and to bring true peace on Earth would likely never be able to be discovered through the external world. The trajectory has to be reversed to know the source, the Tao. And that source is not somewhere *out there*, but rather it is the source of our very being. We must look inward. In the Tao Te Ching, Lao-tzu speaks about this return to the source:

> *Empty yourself of everything.*
> *Let the mind become still.*
> *The ten thousand things rise and fall while*
> *the self watches their return.*
> *They grow and flourish and then return*
> *to the source.*
> *Returning to the source is stillness, which is*
> *the way of nature.*[6]

Our return, according to Lao-tzu, is a return to the Tao of stillness (wu chi), which is the essential nature of the universe in its original state. This return can never happen if we continue to allow our pure awareness to be overpowered by the gravitational pull of the external world. Returning to the source requires us to realign our gaze within and begin to walk the internal path, our true return home.

The internal trajectory of t'ai chi is skillfully harnessed through meditative practices and contemplation. T'ai chi ch'uan, for example, is an internal motion of return, where over time the practitioner harmonizes the yin and yang within themselves to come back into resonance with the Tao in stillness, wu chi. The t'ai chi ch'uan practitioner, and other meditation practitioners, go through the whole gamut of Tao in reverse, from the ten thousand things to wu chi. This is not a creation of a world and identity, but rather a deconstruction. This process in Hinduism is known through Shiva, the destructive principle in the Trimurti of gods: Brahma the creator, Vishnu the preserver, and Shiva the destroyer. Though we could say macrocosmically when the manifest universe has its own time to return to the source, then this is the process of Shiva as well. But microcosmically on an individual level, Shiva destroys your world, your identity, and what is left is the undifferentiated consciousness of Brahman.

Shiva represents the deconstruction of the world you've created in your mind. Shiva destroys all the superimpositions you project onto life so that you can see with your unstained pure awareness. The illusion of *maya* in Hinduism is the world we create in our mind due to how we measure reality according to our conditioning between "this" and "that," which basically means how we discern the reality we are experiencing subjectively into a dichotomy of black-and-white thinking according to the socialization we endured (more on maya later). Shiva deconstructs that illusion so that you can begin to return to Brahman, Tao. In the same way, from a Taoist perspective, the spiritual aspirant engaged in the internal path begins to deconstruct their own world because one's awareness is not entangled with external energy. So the reverse movement of t'ai chi is not the end of the universe, but, instead, it is the end of the world as you know it.

Your alignment with the Tao depends on your return to stillness, the source, and the way of nature. Stillness is your natural constitution, and only in it will you experience the Tao in all life, both within and without. Residing in the stillness of Tao (wu chi) gives you the sense faculty of seeing and feeling the infinite in the ten thousand things, as Chuang-tzu explained.

You are truthfully the hub of the wheel, the emptiness of the bellows. From the meontological state of Tao, you are one with the Tao, and its power is your power. The *I* has dissolved, making one's localization of consciousness an aperture for the Tao to express itself, not *you* as an individual expressing yourself. This power of Tao that sets everything in motion is not something acquired from the external world, but rather it is a power discovered not on the mountaintop but instead in the lowest of places—within.

THE CHARACTER OF RETURN

The predominant character trait of the externally possessed is a drive to succeed and conquer based on self-interest and self-preservation. Our worldview couldn't be otherwise since our awareness is entangled with the external world. This may be the case for the external motion of awareness, but what about the motion of return?

The fundamental position of Taoism is opposite to the world as we know it. Instead of seeking the high places within society, Taoism suggests a movement back to the low places in life that many ordinary people abhor. The character trait of reversal, then, is humility. Taoism can essentially be called the humble path, especially considering that the two main texts of the Tao Te Ching and Chuang-tzu are teachings of humility, radical humility. Lao-tzu teaches that there is a power in the low places, and it is actually where one is in harmony with the Tao. Water is used as an analogy because water always seeks the low places, but, paradoxically, it is the most powerful force in nature. Water's nature is soft and lucid, yet it can wear away the hardness of rock. Likewise, humility seeks the low places and is soft and lucid, but it is paradoxically the most powerful psychological disposition, having the ability to soften the most hardened of hearts.

We sadly live in a world where humility is confused with humiliation. In a world driven externally, humility's value often goes unrecognized. However, it is always there, overcoming the hardened personalities of our world. The humble sage is always in the background awaiting our return. Humility, then, is the character of the hub of the wheel.

It is a state of quiet poise and equanimity that allows one to deal efficaciously with whatever presents itself in life. This is why humility is of paramount importance in martial arts. With it, you harness the ability to deal with the obstacles that are presented with grace. Humility, being the hub, is our center of gravity and where all power is derived from. This power is not derived the other way around, which has unfortunately become the normal view.

Humility is the meontological state of consciousness of the Tao. Only through it can we be one with the Tao. Humility is a state of nothingness, where our pure awareness perceives the world from the stillness of wu chi, with nothing coloring consciousness. You see the world as it honestly is, not how you think it is. Unfortunately, not many people in the world see the world like this. This is evident through the belittling of humility. One without this trait cannot truly function, and a world without humility is completely blind.

None of this is new though. The world has always been blind, fooled by the belief in separation. For this reason, Taoism runs counter to the status quo. It seems to have always been this way. Taoism in its historical context was a critique of Confucianism during the Warring States period of China (something I will discuss at length in chapter two). And Taoism critiques not only Confucianism but any form of socialization that attempts to cultivate the individual to suit its own ends. Taoism is about a return to the uncarved block, our true nature. It criticizes self-cultivation for good reason (discussed more in chapter two). As the world continually goes mad, generation after generation, chasing its own tail, Taoism is always there.

Taoism essentially is a technology for reclaiming our health and sanity. Its application depends on you realizing the difference between the way of socialization and the way of nature. This can only be realized through a return to the source via an embodiment of humility. As the world's inhabitants continue to climb mountaintop after mountaintop in conflict with one another, you've descended into the valley to sit quietly by a stream. As the masses exhaust themselves in striving, you've found quiet contentment in the Tao, the way of harmony. When we reverse the trajectory of motion from the ten thousand things to wu chi, then we become that pure reflection of the Tao.

THE HUMAN MODEL OF THE WHOLE

Since the birth of the universe, from the nothingness of wu chi to the motion of t'ai chi through yin and yang unto the ten thousand things, the human being and other life-forms stand as a representation and reflection of the whole. The big bang did not end billions of years ago; it is still happening within you, and you are the conscious receiver of all of those forces exploding billions of years ago. As philosopher Alan Watts is known to have once said, "You are the big bang, the original force of the universe, coming on as whoever you are."

All of the energy and potentiality residing in the void of wu chi has coalesced within all life-forms in the world, from the simplest to the most complex. Everything is endowed with an energetic signature, some geometrically measurable and others far more complex and intricate. We human beings find ourselves in the far-more-complex-and-intricate category somewhat, for the sheer fact that we are a higher form of consciousness on this planet that have the ability to be conscious of this whole process of Tao. Other life-forms and sentient life, like a dog, are not aware of this process, but we could say they are a pure expression of the Tao because they don't have these more complex intellectual faculties that tend to disconnect us from the source. The ego, for instance, is a good example of this disconnection due to intellectual processes.

In Taoist literature, though, there is an understanding that a human being is a complete representation of the whole. Our higher state of consciousness is a perfect representation of the whole to experience itself subjectively through numerous beings. The big bang's forces and energy coalesce within a human being, making us a model of integration of the whole, the Tao. In the later teachings of Lao-tzu known as the Hua Hu Ching, he states:

> *A human being is a model of the integration of yin and yang, with physical energy manifesting as the body and subtle energy manifesting as the mind and spirit. Further, the ancients referred to these three aspects of the universe as Heaven (symbolized by three solid lines) which is yang, Earth (symbolized by three broken lines) which is yin, and Man (symbolized by Tai Chi) which is integration of yin and yang.[7]*

We are the third aspect of the universe where all of the fundamental forces of the whole emanate out from the center (keeping in mind the hub and wheel analogy). The Tao essentially expands and flows outward from the center creating the ten thousand things (manifest world). We could say we are at the end of that organic process, but a more accurate statement is we are where that process is now in its current state. We can only speculate as to where organic life is heading. Though we do know for sure in its current state a human being is that third aspect, the perfect integration of yin and yang.

The three aspects—Heaven (yang), Earth (yin), and human— are interestingly related to procreation when we consider that the sexual union of male and female creates new life. None of us could be here otherwise, and that is also the case for the creation of the entire universe. The interplay of yin and yang creates life, from the birth of the universe to the birth of a human. We are a reflection of that process on an energetic level. We continue to set the universe in motion or, more precisely perhaps, expand the universe from the center through procreation.

We are a fractal reflection of the whole in an infinite potentiality within the void of the Tao. On all levels, this is happening. Hinduism takes this one step further with the time system of the *Yugas*. In the ancient Hindu texts of the Puranas, we first discover the Yugas, a world-age doctrine of four ages. These ages are known as Satya Yuga, Treta Yuga, Dvapara Yuga, and Kali Yuga. These ages span over 8.64 billion years, which makes up a day and night of Brahma, the creator God or principle of creation in Hinduism. This may seem like a long time to us, but this is just another time cycle within an ongoing, infinite process of time through the birth, death, and rebirth process of the universe. That's right, this current universe we are experiencing, from a Hindu perspective, is not the only game in town, nor is it the last. Actually, it's not the first, either, because the concept of a beginning and end are only relevant to linear time as we know it, and so they both dissolve into the eternal vastness of Brahman or Tao.

Birth, death, and rebirth are not isolated to the life forces of the manifest world. They are also reflected on the macrocosmic level. Universes are born and die, only to be reborn again. Essentially, this process reflected in a human being is minuscule to the greater whole.

The warrior prince Arjuna felt exactly the same on the ancient battlefield of Kurukshetra when the godly sage Krishna revealed his real form in the classical Hindu text of the Bhagavad Gita.* We are on the outer layer of that image, which may seem quite small, but as they explain in Vedanta, the Atman (undifferentiated consciousness) in all of us is identical to Brahman, the ultimate reality, and the Tao.

Likewise, the Tao is doing each of us, and yet the ego we believe we are blocks the fundamental forces from using us effectively. Our egos are like dams in a river. The dam is unnatural and blocks the natural flow of the river. Likewise, your ego is unnatural. It is a construct built on an accumulative set of knowledge from the external world and socialization that we mistakenly associate and identify with. The ego is the accumulative self we've put together from external cues and information, not the natural self. The Tao can make use of us when we are open vessels available to receive all of the fundamental forces of the universe.

The perfect integration of the three aspects can only occur when, on an individual level, we have removed the blockage, the ego. Physically and mentally, we have all been endowed as a representation of the whole, the human integration of the three aspects of Heaven (yang), Earth (yin), and human (the perfect integration of yin and yang, t'ai chi). To be as nature intended us, and for the Tao to utilize us, we have to spiritually remove the ego. The Tao utilizes us to express itself through us according to our own psychosomatic makeup. Tao is the way of nature and so always follows what is intrinsic to us. It is not a man-made construct. Naturally, the three aspects follow the nature of the Tao as Lao-tzu explains in the Tao Te Ching:

---

*Arjuna was one of the main protagonists in the Hindu epic the Mahabharata. The Bhagavad Gita is a book within the Mahabharata that depicts a dialogue between Arjuna and Krishna immediately before the Kurukshetra War between the related royal families of the Pandavas and Kauravas, to which Arjuna was a Pandava. Krishna is the eighth avatar of Vishnu, a representation of the supreme Brahman.

The human being follows the earth.

Earth follows heaven.

Heaven follows the Tao.

Tao follows what is natural.[8]

The Tao following what is natural is illustrated through the Taoist concept of *tzu-jan* (自然: Wade-Giles *tzu-jan*; Pinyin *ziran*), "spontaneously of itself," or in other words, its "self-evident nature." Tzu-jan is more commonly known as "naturalness." The organic world is fundamentally natural, and by harmonizing with the natural course of the world, we discover our own self-so nature because we are in alignment with the Tao. Unfortunately, we create all sorts of unnatural systems of belief and control that annihilate this nature in an individual.

We essentially cannot be in harmony with the Tao or express its intrinsic beauty if we can't let go of the materialistic, self-centered beliefs and hypnosis of separation that socialization inculcates within us. We can hardly be natural through control. We must let go of control and the reason we yearn for it, the accumulative sense of self, ego, and identity.

LET GO AND FLOW
WITH THE RIVER OF TAO

The river is a powerful analogy for this process of letting go of ourselves to allow the Tao to make use of us. Actually, the river analogy builds the whole framework of Taoist philosophical and metaphysical understanding. This simple yet, at first, hard-to-comprehend river analogy is the natural science for understanding life and our small part of it.

The secret science of the river analogy is written into the title of the Tao Te Ching. Orientalist and sinologist Arthur Waley translated the title of the Tao Te Ching as *The Way and Its Power.*

The "way" is obviously the Tao, but it is the "power" of the Tao aspect many people leave aside or don't understand thoroughly. The *te* (德: Wade-Giles *te*; Pinyin *de*) of the Tao Te Ching is the power or virtue of the Tao. But the te resides in us; it is up to us to reorient our way of life to accord with the Tao. Then, and only then, will we experience its power and virtue. Te, then, is extremely important for understanding the river analogy. The river analogy will show you what is necessary to align with the Tao and is as follows:

The river of the Tao is always flowing, a constant of life. We are all in that river. But most of us are either holding on to the banks of the river or fighting the current in trying to swim against it. Both attitudes are problematic and destructive. The problem with holding on to the banks of the river is you are stranded; you are not going anywhere and live in constant fear of being swept away. Likewise, the problem with swimming against the current is you'll eventually get tired and drown. For both positions the only realistic action is to let go and trust the river. Once we let go, we discover that the river's power becomes our power. We might not know where the river is taking us, but we are not exhausted in fighting the process, which allows us to develop a deep trust in the process or river. You flow with the river as one with it.

Before I dive into flowing with the river, we need to understand this analogy. The river itself is the Tao. Holding on to the banks of the river is a representation of how we hold on to certain things and experiences in our lives that create unnecessary attachment to things, people, and experiences. This attachment blocks you from living your life naturally. Most people have created a certain life for themselves that has boundaries and essentially is stagnant. We are afraid to let go because of an ingrained fear of uncertainty that has developed due to the illusion that we've created certainty or safety in our lives. Any form of uncertainty in life is avoided by clinging to our worldviews, the banks in the river, so we worry about them getting thrown upside down.

Similarly, swimming against the river represents a somewhat identical problem. The current of the river is always guiding our lives whether we like it or not. We try to swim against the current when we don't like the direction our life is going. We try to control our life as it is in this very moment. But the river's current is constant. Any attempt to fight this current will lead to suffering, and this is what happens on an individual level. We often get ourselves in trouble because we are fighting the circumstances of life. The more we fight, the more we suffer. Unfortunately, many people are so accustomed to fighting the river for control of their lives that they eventually drown from complete exhaustion and burn out.

These control issues are an affliction many people suffer from. We are under the illusion that we are the masters of our fate. But nothing could be further from the truth. We might be able to control a small fragment of our lives, but not in its totality. The river governs our lives and has always done so. We are not in control. That very statement erodes fear in many who are still holding on. But when you understand the river of the Tao is genuinely guiding your life, you naturally let go of the will you thought you needed to gain the kind of control you probably always wanted but never knew existed. This may sound paradoxical to those geared toward the external world of force and control, but this is the way of the Tao, the way of nature. This paradoxical force is the core principle of the river analogy because when you stop fighting the current, the river's power becomes your power. This is te, the power and virtue of the Tao.

In letting go, you flow with the Tao, allowing its current to guide your life without resistance. As the power of lightning follows the path of least resistance, so does the Tao. And if your mind is full of beliefs, opinions, and identity, then you are resistant to the flow of Tao. When we completely let go, we harness te. Without force and control, the Tao can make use of you. This trust in the effortless flow of the river is the fundamental nondoing component of wu-wei. As chapter thirty-seven of the Tao Te Ching states:

Tao abides in non-action,
Yet nothing is left undone.[9]

In letting go of ourselves, the Tao does all without our sense of identity there at all. This is the real sense of effortless action (wu-wei). No planning or contriving is needed for the Tao to run its course. It does all without our input. Te demonstrates how the Tao does us, essentially how it manifests in our life through wu-wei. The t'ai chi movement from the nameless source (wu chi) to the ten thousand things is te. That is the river, the stream of conscious energy constantly flowing through us. We are created to receive this energy radiating from the ultimate reality of the Tao consciously so that we can manifest it through our actions. But the irony is that we need to reverse our trajectory and return to the source to open ourselves for the Tao to move through us. This is the mutual motion of the bidirectional movement of t'ai chi. As

Jacob Needleman explains in the introduction and notes to the Tao Te Ching, "Thus, the movement that leads back to the source is also the opening toward great action in outer life. Virtue is an opening rather than a 'doing.'"[10]

The movement of return is equivalent to ceasing fighting the current to allow yourself to be one with the power of the river. This is the human virtue of the nonvirtuous, not some self-righteous moralistic attitude (I will explain this in later chapters). In brief, morality is built on social rules and values that differ between cultures and nations. These differing moral beliefs are inculcated in an individual that creates an ego with an ingrained agenda based on those moral beliefs. This process warps our nature. We become a social construct of society, but we need to remember that society is man-made.

Socialization is superimposed on our minds, which in turn acts as a blockage to the fundamental forces of Tao. To flow with the river of Tao, to harness the virtue of te, means we need to release these social constraints that fool us into fighting the river. A human being, like any other organism, is designed as a reflection of the Tao. However, humans are innately constricted due to our higher state of intelligence, which can create all sorts of strange ways of thinking and beliefs that disconnect us from the way of nature. The river analogy teaches us that we are a pure expression of Tao, not in what we do but rather in who we are, or more correctly, subtract the *who* and instead we are a pure expression of Tao *as* we are.

THE ORGANIC PATTERN
OF NATURAL HARMONY

The natural beauty of the world is only possible by virtue of a universal order that gives rise to an organic pattern intrinsic in nature. Innately within a seed is the whole pattern of a plant, with leaves, stem, fruit, and everything else necessary for it to exist. Likewise, within the source of the nothingness of Tao is the whole vast array of patterns that we call our universe. The river of Tao, from wu chi to the ten thousand things, conforms to a cosmic organic pattern. This is the natural course of the universe that we find in the wind, leaves, wood, our nerves, and even the movement of the planets, and more.

From the microcosm to the macrocosm, there is an order to the universe that all life naturally follows. This pattern found on all levels of life breeds a harmony that allows symmetry to happen in the universe. Everything has an organic pattern, either distinct or indistinct, because we all come from the source of the Tao, the seed of life.

In Taoism this organic pattern is known in Chinese as *li* (理: Wade-Giles *li*; Pinyin *li*). Don't confuse this li with Confucian li (禮: Wade-Giles *li*; Pinyin *li*), which is based on correct understanding and practices of rites and ceremonies. The Confucian concept of li has no relevance to Taoism or to the harmony of nature. Taoist li is translated as the natural markings in jade, grain in wood, and fiber in muscle. Before his untimely death in 1973, philosopher Alan Watts explained li beautifully in his last book *Tao: The Watercourse Way*:

> The Chinese call this kind of beauty the following of li, an ideogram which referred originally to the grain in jade and wood, and which [Joseph] Needham translates as "organic pattern," although it is more generally understood as the "reason" or "principle" of things. Li is the pattern of behavior which comes about when one is in accord with the Tao, the watercourse of nature.[11]

The pattern of li is found everywhere in nature and also in the outer universe. If we look into the grain of wood, the markings of a tortoise shell, the skin of an elephant, the spiral pattern of a sunflower, our own palms, and so on, we discover the organic pattern of li. Even the spiral formation of the Milky Way galaxy exhibits li on the macrocosmic level. Remarkably, li in some cases is mathematically fixed to the Golden Ratio of the Fibonacci sequence discovered by the thirteenth-century Italian mathematician Leonardo Fibonacci. Li essentially is an energetic signature or blueprint within nature that evokes harmony.

The mineral, plant, and animal kingdoms exhibit li naturally. Those three kingdoms are naturally harmonious. All three naturally follow the course of nature because every organism within those kingdoms can be nothing other than what they are. A horse's nature is this, a rock's nature is that, and so on. Nothing can disrupt their intrinsic li. The intrinsic pattern of a bodhi leaf cannot willingly change its fundamental pattern. It just does what bodhi leaves do, and that is why it is harmonious with everything else.

Those three kingdoms naturally move with the river of Tao and obviously have no inclination or capability to fight the current. The human kingdom, on the other hand, is a completely different story. We are the most complex organism on this planet because of our higher intelligence. This higher intelligence should be beneficial, but often it is a hindrance. The reason is that many of us lack the awareness to stop fighting the river of Tao. We don't know that in letting go, we will align with the Tao, and its power will become our power. Naturally, both biologically and psychologically, we are perfectly adapted to the world due to our li. But the way our li is discovered is in the same way other organisms function—by flowing with the river of Tao.

Our overidentification with an accumulative sense of self and our desire to control our life based on that ego disrupts our natural harmony with all life. Unfortunately, we are not a human expression of Tao, but rather a human expression of a self-image we've conjured in our minds. As a result, a human being finds it difficult to harmonize with everything else. We are out of sync. This is best illustrated through our inability to accept other people and also by our plundering of natural resources to appease our insatiable desire for personal comforts. We take way more from nature than necessary, leaving a desert in our wake. Moderation is a concept that we've struggled to comprehend since large-scale societies were born.

A natural, simple life is a surefire way for discovering your li. But your li is discovered not in *who* you are but rather in *what* you are. The discovery of your li is complex. Only by letting go and allowing the river's power to become our power (te), can we discover our li. By not resisting the river and instead moving with it effortlessly (wu-wei), we will live our li.

Being a more complex organism means that our li isn't as simple as a pattern in a leaf (though, keep in mind, biologically we discover li in our palms, for example). Sure, the same organic pattern of li within the ecosystem is the same intelligence found in our nerves, muscles, and senses, but ultimately li is also found in our cognitive functions and psychology. In understanding the river analogy, we can now comprehend why our li is at the level of our psychological functions. Essentially, li is a pattern we have innately within our minds.

The li we discover through our psychological constitution and disposition is revealed only when we let go and move with the river. Li is a result of harnessing te and living by wu-wei. Our li is always there, like the grain in wood, but we have to get out of our own way to recognize it. Li is our pure reflection of the Tao, our intrinsic beauty. And just as different trees have different leaf patterns, so do different humans have their own unique patterns.

The law of li is constant; however, the pattern it produces is in accord with the harmony of Tao. When we are flowing harmoniously with the river of Tao, we discover our li. This discovery occurs because we realize by moving with the river what our organism is innately adapted to—essentially what has a natural resonance within our minds, what comes to us effortlessly as opposed to feeling labored.

The socialization we've all experienced doesn't allow us to grow as nature intended. Hence, many never discover our natural li. With all sorts of distractions and social ideologies vying for your attention, it is increasingly harder to flow with the river to discover your li. But when you do discover it, you will naturally yearn for your natural environment. That may mean surrounding yourself with music because your organic pattern is adapted to music, for example. Just as our bodies are perfectly adapted to the terrain of the planet, so, too, our organic pattern is adapted to the environment or atmosphere that corresponds with our li. We are just like a plant in this sense. A plant flourishes in its natural environment, and we, too, flourish in our li's natural environment.

We come into accord with the world when we discover our li. But we have to begin to act as nature is, reverse our trajectory, and turn our gaze back within to the source of Tao. Nature is harmonious because each of its components follows its own li, and together with other manifestations of Tao, other parts of nature, they flow together as one in the river. Humans are also nature, and we authentically harmonize with everything else when we follow our own unique li. By flowing with the river of Tao we recalibrate with the world and move with it as one. In doing so, we reveal an essential principle in Taoist philosophy known in Chinese as *ying* (應: Wade-Giles *ying*; Pinyin *ying*). Ying means "mutual resonance and interdependence." Mutual resonance and interdependence are only possible by following your li, essentially by following the Tao. The effect of li is ying.

By following our organic pattern (li), we harmonize with the world and inspire others; this is ying. Your li is like the flame of a candle, and the light it gives off is ying. It enlightens the world around you. When you experience ying, you are a complete reflection of the Tao for it to express itself. You end up giving off a natural radiance by letting go so that your will aligns with the Tao, but you cannot force this to happen through your own will or personality. The effect of ying is when your virtue shines. But, as you've probably gathered already, ying is not experienced by moral grandstanding or righteousness. Rather, it is experienced by seeking the low places on our way back to the source. You are as nature is, not what society has trained you to be or think. Anything externally imposed on you, training you according to the social thoughtform, can never be your li or produce an effect of ying. Both li and ying are intrinsic characteristics of the river of Tao, and we discover them within ourselves when we are a perfect representation of the river.

Socialization does not endow you with li and ying from the external world because they are already natural within you. Just as the artist endows a blank canvas with paint, so do we endow the external world with life. Our li is innately in the world, producing ying. This process is best illustrated through art—music, for example. An individual discovers their li is music, and then by following that path, they eventually become a well-known artist. When a musician is on the stage in concert in front of a crowd or when people hear their music, people are inspired and moved by the musician's li. This is mutual resonance and interdependence, ying. The musician has a harmonizing effect with their environment where people gravitate toward them and are inspired by them. This is the musician's virtue, te. This whole process of te emanating through li to produce ying is what helps others to realize their own innate potential, their own li.

Ying is this harmonizing effect, fueling inspiration in the heart of humanity. But inspiration is not the only effect of ying. The purest expression of the river of Tao is the Taoist sage or spiritual master. The sage is definitely inspirational for those with their ears open and hearts attuned to the Tao, but that is not really their ying effect. Wisdom is their ying. We gain wisdom from the sage that allows us to understand the nature of ourselves and the universe we inhabit. The whole guru-disciple relationship is the result of ying. The guru has realized their true nature and so harbors wisdom, which energetically pulls people toward the guru who are attuned to the guru's li. The guru's te, virtue, has a gravitational pull that attracts people seeking a deeper life. But no matter whether it is a sage or a musician, the underlying process of li and ying is the same in principle, though different in appearance.

None of us are principally different. We are all a stream of the Tao when we reverse our trajectory. We are all an aperture of the universe to express itself. We are built to receive, contain, and transform the power of Tao, making our life a complete expression of it. Tao, te, li, and ying are the complete process of expression, and this process exists on all levels from wu chi through the movement of t'ai chi, with yin and yang on to the ten thousand things. Our life is designed to be a reflection of the Tao because that is our nature. Nothing else will bring us ultimate fulfillment. We chase our tails day after day on the social and cultural treadmill, which destroys our minds and maddens our hearts, just as Lao-tzu explains in chapter twelve of the Tao Te Ching, "The chase and the hunt madden our hearts."

Most of us have little to no awareness of the river of Tao, the stream of consciousness waiting to guide our lives. Everything we do with a conditioned mind cuts us off from the source. We may pray, write books about it, go to church, and so on, but those things are all closed off from the Tao because they are all based on man-made beliefs and built on separation, not the way of nature. What we believe, including the ideologies we follow, are obstacles on the path to freedom. In Lao-tzu's time, it was no different. He had to contest with the Confucian indoctrination project built around him. In the end, the obstacles on our path are not the components of society, but rather socialization itself. The birth of Taoism was a reaction to this socialization experiment thrust on the people during China's Warring States period.

2

Taoism's Critique of Confucianism and Socialization

During the Warring States period (475–221 BCE), many different schools of thought were born. The classical period of Chinese philosophy is known as the *Hundred Schools of Thought*, and it flourished from the sixth century BCE to 221 BCE, during the Spring and Autumn period (771–476 BCE). Many philosophies from this time are either lost or only studied as a subject in academia rather than practiced. However, Taoism and Confucianism have survived since that period and are both the most influential philosophies of China and Far East Asia in general.

Though, to be sure, Confucianism is the prevailing school of thought for the masses. Taoism, on the other hand, has always been in the background and only followed by the most peculiar of society. Even though China is communist, Confucianism is so deeply entrenched in the psyche and culture of the people. A foreign ideology, such as communism, can't eradicate that type of culture and thinking within a few generations. For that reason, Confucianism has been tolerated since the Cultural Revolution. Taoism, on the other hand, has experienced persecution since that time, when many Taoists fled to Taiwan. Buddhism suffered the same fate when we look back at the atrocities that happened in Tibet. Both Taoism and Buddhism suffered at the hands of the Cultural Revolution because of both traditions' spiritual nature, which runs counter to communist ideology. Confucianism, on the other hand, survived due to its sociopolitical nature.

Regardless, Confucianism has usually been the prevailing school of thought in China, and Taoism has mostly remained as a hard-to-grasp teaching that only a minority of the population understands and follows. There are many reasons for this lack of understanding, but the main reason is a bias we have as humans in how we should act and behave in a social setting. This bias is fundamentally flawed (more on this soon). Most cultures have this bias, and it began when agrarian societies and large-scale societies started to form. Taoism, on the other hand, was a way of life pre-society. Both philosophies and the flawed human bias most people have can be explained by two metaphors that have culturally defined Chinese thought in general for twenty-five hundred years: the carving and polishing metaphor of Confucius (孔子: Wade-Giles *K'ung-fu-tzu* or *K'ung-tzu*; Pinyin *Kongfuzi* or *Kongzi*; 551–479 BCE) and the uncarved block metaphor of Lao-tzu. These are completely different perspectives of the world.

THE SELF-CULTIVATION MODEL

The carving and polishing metaphor of Confucius is a philosophy based on the self-cultivation of the individual and also the society. This philosophy spawns from the flawed human prejudice that influences how the Tao is thought to be. According to Confucius, the Tao is something we experience and come into alignment with when we cultivate the individual according to certain rules and structure in society. Essentially Confucius believed the Tao is something induced through order. As if the Tao is something we externally bring into our life rather than it being natural to everything.

Confucianism is built on this idea of inducing the Tao through the strict morality and rules we should follow (more on this later). Confucius believed we are naturally beasts and so we need to be trained like any other domestic animal. This is the subtle human bias many cultures live by that I was alluding to earlier; hence we have a vast plethora of religions and moral philosophies based on the concept that we are supposedly uncultured beasts. By following Confucian morality, we will supposedly become a *junzi* (君子: Wade-Giles *chün-tzu*; Pinyin *junzi*), a "superior man/gentleman." The "man" part is literal, too, because Confucius didn't believe a woman could be superior in the Confucian sense.

We ought to cultivate ourselves on an individual level according to Confucian morality because apparently humans are inherently flawed, and so goodness, humility, compassion, forgiveness, and so forth can only be cultivated, not naturally come by. As a result, Confucius structured society to propagate his moral norms so that people were socially inculcated with his beliefs. The individual, then, becomes a reflection of society based on what is socially accepted.

The problem with the carving and polishing model is, who's to say we are beasts from birth? Who's to say we are not inherently good? Who's to say we need social cultivation? This socialization model is in complete contrast to the way of nature. This is where Taoism comes in with its natural methodology.

THE NATURAL MODEL

Lao-tzu explains in the Tao Te Ching that we need to return to the unhewn wood, the uncarved block. The uncarved block stands as a metaphor for our raw, pure nature, that which was natural before it was touched by the human hand and mind of the world. Taoism, thus, is a natural methodology where the Tao is natural to the world and not something we can cultivate or induce. The Taoist way of thinking is a complete backflip to the common bias that we are beasts in need of cultivation. Innate within our nature is fundamental goodness, compassion, forgiveness, empathy, and humility. Those traits are not something you can cultivate according to Taoism; they are intrinsic in your being just like wood is intrinsic to a tree.

The uncarved block metaphor suggests that we are not beasts at all, but rather it is the socialization process we all endure that turns us into beasts, essentially warping our nature. From the Taoist perspective, we are fundamentally good, and this goodness is destroyed when we go through a self-cultivation method. Lao-tzu explained that by following Confucian morality, we destroy our innate morality imbued with the qualities of compassion, forgiveness, empathy, love, and humility. Actually, this form of social-moral cultivation critiqued by Taoism can be applied to any society and culture of our time or throughout history.

No matter in what age, the socialization process we endure turns us into beasts according to Taoism. Education, culture, society, and religion all shape our raw nature and, in doing so, disconnect us from the Tao, the way of nature. The way of nature is how nature is in its pure form, not nature after the human hand and mind have dealt with it. Some may say we need education, at least language, so we can communicate, and Lao-tzu wouldn't totally disagree. But he would warn us to know when enough is enough.

Early Taoist communities still had language. They also had a form of education, but the difference is that it was framed through nature and not the other way around. Everything arose naturally according to an individual's li, which brought ying into the community. But where Taoism departs from Confucianism, and organized societies in general, is morality. Lao-tzu explained that an external system of moral principles destroys our nature and turns us into beasts. We are innately good and so we shouldn't carve the unhewn wood too much, if at all. This view might be shocking for many people, but this is the way of nature.

The Tao Te Ching, essentially, is a manual for unraveling ourselves from Confucian morality so we can be natural again. We must return to the uncarved block, our authentic selves, so that we can harmonize with nature. Even though most of us go through the carving and polishing process, there is still hope because there is still wood. The nature of wood is still within a carved and polished piece, though granted a little warped, but nevertheless the wood's basic nature is still intact. So a return to our nature is possible, but we have to reverse the trajectory of our awareness and look within rather than being dictated to by external moral principles in general.

Taoism, being the way of nature, runs counter to any social structure and ideology. This counter view is one of the most misunderstood aspects of Taoism, especially due to the misunderstanding and mishandling of Taoism by new age spirituality and Western minds influenced by poor translations and other religions.

WHY CONFUCIAN MORALITY DESTROYS THE TAO

When many people think of Taoism, they believe it is primarily a philosophy about wu-wei and living in harmony with nature. As a result, being in the zone and effortless living, or being in the flow, are attributed to Taoism. And there is nothing wrong with this view; they do belong to Taoism, but this is not the complete picture nor an accurate description.

In my fifteen-plus years of teaching Eastern philosophy, I often witness a lot of glazed eyes that are either confused or disinterested when I mention that Taoism is in part a critique of Confucianism. They are confused because most people believe Confucius was this noble sage, and they are disinterested because this knowledge conflicts with their incorrect view of Taoism, and so it is not what they want to hear. Sure, the way of nature and the concept of the Tao predates the Warring States period and Confucianism in China, but it was inherently used to critique humanity's evolution into large-scale societies and socially accepted systems of morality such as Confucianism.

Fake Sincerity

Taoism is against a particular fake or false sincerity that is promoted and practiced by Confucians. Confucian morality is designed to teach a sincerity within us that supposedly leads us to being human. Once again, Confucian morality implies that we were primitive and uncultured before the existence of Confucianism. Essentially, Confucianism is an education and domestic program designed to train people to be sincere and natural. Confucianism, being a self-cultivation model, is a socially imposed system that people are supposed to treat as if it is the natural way to be. Confucianism essentially trains us mere beasts to be human, and then we can be natural. But Taoism exposes the falsity and hypocrisy of this sincerity and the notion of being natural as a result of Confucian morality.

Taoism's critique reveals that this sincerity model can lead to all sorts of pathologies. This is all due to how sincerity based on Confucian naturalness affects our mental health long-term. The reason for this is the *regime of sincerity,* as philosophers Hans-Georg Moeller and Paul J. D'Ambrosio put it, which leads to an overidentification with one's role. Confucian morality, as the regime of sincerity, is designed for us to live our social role genuinely, no matter whether it conflicts with our innate nature. And in Confucianism these roles are often hierarchical and run counter to morality itself when we take a closer look.

The Confucian regime of sincerity is a complex structure of rules and roles based on a hierarchical order. These roles are not as simple as the roles a mother or father plays according to their natural constitution. There are still the roles of mother and father in Confucianism, but those roles and every other role are entangled in a complex web of rules and regulations. This complex set of rules and regulations consists of gender bias, the bound feet of women, filial piety, sleeping in certain positions according to one's role, eating in certain positions, and on and on. Yes, Confucius had a weird opinion of women, and he actually advised them to bind their feet because this is what was required to align with his own twisted idea of nature.

Confucius wouldn't have a place in our modern world. Or maybe I'm wrong; he might have a place because his emphasis on political correctness, virtue signaling, and intellectual imperialism would be applauded by some groups doing the same. If he could just tweak his pious arrogance to accommodate the sensibilities of the present day, then he would be a modern hero championing the mindlessness so common in our modern, unstable world. Nevertheless, this morality was Confucius's idea of what is natural and how the Tao is induced in the world. In the Confucian text known as *The Doctrine of the Mean*, Confucian morality and the regime of sincerity are explained as the natural order of the universe that we ought to submit to: "Sincerity is the dao/way of nature/heaven; making it sincere is the dao/way of humankind."[1]

According to *The Doctrine of the Mean*, you should be like the stars, moon, and sun, all following their natural courses. But ironically, Confucian morality with all of its unnatural rules and regulations is supposedly related to the natural course of the heavens and is the "nature" we should follow to be natural. We essentially have to be at ease with our bound feet and all. And if you don't commit to this system, then you are not considered human because you are not natural. This is backward logic and the complete opposite view to Taoism. First of all, the course of the stars, moon, and planets are natural of themselves (tzu-jan); and secondly, no man-made system can replicate organic nature because it is of a secondary nature based on a subjective, conditioned view.

Confucius's view, then, is artificial and essentially an external system that can never be natural. Confucian morality is fundamentally a man-made system imposed on us based on an idea that arose in the mind of Confucius. So to commit to such a system can only produce artificiality within those who follow it. As a result, innate character traits such as sincerity, humility, and compassion are all framed through this imposed morality. Only by making these innate traits align with this morality will they be natural. This type of backward logic is detrimental to the followers of Confucianism. The psychological damage that Confucianism has produced is still visible in Far East Asia today, especially since the prevalent cognitive style has been fashioned on this viewpoint. Three main problems are produced by the regime of sincerity that may exist within all cultures but are prevalent within the strict domestic program of Confucian morality: stress, worthlessness, and vanity.

Stress

Stress is a natural byproduct of Confucianism. People must be constantly paranoid about their position in society and if they are enacting their role correctly. According to the hierarchy of roles in this belief system, we are always self-conscious of our social appearance and status. We must play our role perfectly or we face scrutiny and criticism from society. And to have the perfect social appearance and status according to one's role is overwhelmingly stressful. There are just far too many details to remember to be a Confucian. We have to be constantly mindful of how we talk, sit, act, and sleep, yes even sleep. What position you sleep in should correspond to your role. I'm not sure if anyone truthfully follows this sleeping mandate considering that to sleep one must be comfortable most of the time, which is a natural sense, not an artificial position of what is comfortable. Stress is inescapable within such a system. The stress produced by our paranoia of following our role well coincides with the second problem produced by the regime of sincerity.

Worthlessness

The feeling of worthlessness is another byproduct. This is a no-brainer when we consider roles and status. Roles in Confucianism are typically hierarchical. Invariably, most of us find ourselves in a lower position within society, and even those in an upper position of authority find themselves still subordinate to a superior. This is usually the case with most roles, no matter social or familial. This is intensified through this belief system because of the complex hierarchical structures of roles. Confucius wants you to identify with your role completely, no matter what position you are in. This view is inherently problematic because the role you submit to and play unconsciously makes you feel worthless according to your position in the hierarchical structure.

We willingly accept worthlessness as a result of internalizing inferiority. The roles we play cannot but have this effect considering most of us are in a lower position. Hans-Georg Moeller takes this a step further and calls this an "institutionalized internalized inferiority complex." Confucian morality cultivates this inferiority complex, leading the masses to feel worthless, even though, in reality, this feeling only applies to their role, not to who they genuinely are. However in this system, your role is who you should be and essentially believed to be who you truly are. This is the regime of sincerity. This mind-boggling worldview is inherently problematic.

Vanity

Just as identifying with lower roles produces worthlessness, on the opposite end of the spectrum, identifying with higher positions of superiority produces vanity. A Confucian position of superiority breeds and institutionalizes conceit. Any hierarchical structure produces vanity because superior roles are thought to be high in status, which supposedly reflects one's virtue. Nothing could be further from the truth, especially when we consider how roles are set up in Confucianism. An individual in a so-called higher position has an institutionalized and internalized superiority complex, which leads to conceit. As John Dalberg-Acton, the Catholic historian, politician, and writer, wrote in 1887, "Power tends to corrupt, and absolute power corrupts absolutely. Great men are almost always bad men."[2]

When we create artificial roles measured by lower or upper positions, only worthlessness or vanity can be produced. This answers the age-old conundrum of why those who attain a position of authority begin to at least slightly change; they have embodied their role, which is measured as high on the scale of status within society. Many of us have witnessed this firsthand when a colleague or friend gets a promotion or becomes a boss. And on the other end of the spectrum, we have witnessed or may have experienced being demoted, fired, or undermined by a superior in front of colleagues, which in turn instills worthlessness inside us. The result of either upper or lower positions is actually negative and against the natural course of life. Both are measurements according to a social system, no matter whether that is Confucianism or any other flawed belief system. Such measurements aren't natural. This makes the whole structure of Confucian hierarchy flawed.

As Moeller and D'Ambrosio explain:

Confucian morality brings about what it tries to get rid of—namely, falsity, hypocrisy, and selfishness. It creates the very problems it claims to resolve. Confucian moral demands are, to use more contemporary parlance, tied to social constructs. And rather than simply demanding conformity with such social constructs, a Confucian ethics demands the impossible—that one "naturalize" the social by personally substantiating family relationships and political roles established by the structures of a social order. This impossible demand is to sincerely make one's own what is not one's own to begin with, or in the words of the *Analects*, "what has been passed on" to oneself.[3]

A subtle form of instability and suffering result from the regime of sincerity imposed on society. Under Confucian morality, people naturally develop pathologies that affect the world. A real sense of madness becomes the norm, with nearly everyone suffering the same affliction. Psychopathic and sociopathic norms lead to a psychopathic and sociopathic world.

The heart of the pathology is that this belief system is fundamentally paradoxical because it attempts to naturalize what is not natural. Confucian morality itself is not intrinsic, yet we ought to treat it as natural as the movement of the wind according to Confucius. Binding our feet, sleeping a certain way, and embodying our social roles are all supposed to be somehow inherent to life. As Alan Watts said, "Life is wiggly," and yet we are trying to superimpose straight rigid lines onto nature as if they were natural in the first place. That would be similar to someone who has plastic surgery. The person who gets plastic surgery is trying to look younger but distorts nature to achieve that goal. Personally, they may be pleased with the outcome, but they aren't fooling anybody; we can sense that something isn't quite right. Similarly, Taoists observed this whole Confucian naturalization project and could immediately sense something was off. We can never naturalize what is not natural. We have a word for that, *artificial*.

Taoism is about indicating the pathologies that develop under the Confucian regime of sincerity and why we need to return to the genuine, natural way as it is, the Tao. The Tao Te Ching, then, acts as a manual to reclaim our health and sanity by returning to the true way of nature. Chapter eighteen of the Tao Te Ching explains how human virtue according to Confucius is an expression of the decay of pathology:

> When the great Dao is dispensed with,
> then there is humanity and righteousness.
> When knowledge and smartness come out,
> then there is great falsity.[4]

Knowledge and smartness in chapter eighteen means what is morally correct according to Confucianism. Gia-Fu Feng and Jane English's translation, for example, substitutes "knowledge and smartness" for "wisdom and intelligence." A lot of people who read the Tao Te Ching get confused because they think, for example, how could wisdom and intelligence be bad? If you have no context then you don't know. This is why it is extremely important to understand any knowledge in its historical context without appropriating it to suit ourselves. So we shouldn't misinterpret knowledge and smartness from a modernist perspective. They are actually related to Confucian morality. Nevertheless, in chapter eighteen we see what is lost by trying to naturalize something artificial.

Instead of allowing families and societies to have autonomy and grow naturally, Confucian morality steps in with its rules and regulations and distorts our nature. Does this sound familiar? Every external system does this in some way, some with good intentions and others more about totalitarianism. No matter whether it is democracy, communism, Marxism, or the Catholic Church, they all seek to mold and warp our natures to suit their own ideology. The difference between the Warring States period of China and now is that there are far more ideologies in the present day competing for your obedience. It is the same underlying motivation; they've just gone through the passage of time and have continually evolved to suit the ever-changing human social dynamic. And the further we've gone down this path, the more distant the Tao is to us. That is why in chapter eighteen of the Tao Te Ching, it states that the Tao is forgotten (in Gia-Fu Feng and Jane English's translation)—actually that it is dispensed with for some artificial world of hyper rules and regulations.

The more we go through a socialization process of any form, the more we lose contact with the Tao. Even though the Tao can never leave you, as it is the ultimate reality, it can be forgotten to the point that we believe our social norms are natural and cultivate us mere beasts. This unbelievable cycle began with such moral systems as Confucianism. Essentially, Taoism's underlying point is that life was better before all of these societal rules and traditions were imposed on us. We lost the way because we became domesticated and socialized creatures. The simple way of the ancients, the early Taoists, is completely forgotten and, as a result, the Tao is a distant memory for those engaged in creating a self-image, a role to adapt to Confucian morality.

THE WISE ROBBER
AND THE FOOLISH SAGE

In chapter twenty-nine of the Chuang-tzu, Robber Chih (盜跖: Wade-Giles *Chih*; Pinyin *Zhi*), a criminal mastermind, tries to explain to Confucius that life was better before Confucianism. This chapter is about the hypocrisy of the claim that Confucianism is rooted in any kind of natural state. Chapter twenty-nine of the

Chuang-tzu is one of the least known chapters; however it is very important for understanding the Taoist mentality opposed to Confucian morality. This chapter is a great representation of the humor of Chuang-tzu. Humor, along with humility, are two key characteristics of Taoism. But people who are easily offended due to their modern sensibilities—such as moralists and social justice warriors wielding their worldview upon other people—won't understand the story. For example, Robber Chih is depicted in the story as eating minced human liver in the afternoon for a snack. For this reason, and many others within the Chuang-tzu, the story is a parody with a spiritual significance for the individual. Understanding the humor of the Chuang-tzu is essential for any Taoist.

There have been many interpretations of chapter twenty-nine by untrained minds. For example, the anti-Confucian readings of the Robber Chih story that were reached during the Cultural Revolution of Maoist China, in accordance with the schematic dialectical materialism of the time, were that Robber Chih was a leader of a revolutionary slave revolt that challenged the ancient feudal system of Confucianism. Robber Chih was depicted in popular political material as a rebel and champion of the oppressed who triumphed over Confucianism.

This interpretation is somewhat valid, but when you understand that the story is a parody, you can no longer agree with this Maoist interpretation of Robber Chih because, in the end, he is not an outright hero. Instead, he is presented in the story as a carnivalesque figure, even though he is outwardly attractive. He is the complete opposite of moralist hypocrisies and social conventions. His very nature subjugates Confucian morality and the embodiment of social values.

Robber Chih best represents Taoism as a critique of Confucianism. He exposes the flaws of Confucian morality and any social system that aims to cultivate individuals according to their beliefs. Robber Chih has zero tolerance for unnatural systems that seek to cultivate naturalness, making innocent people believe the system is natural. He opposed any such system and points to a time when we followed nature and never forgot the Tao:

> In the age of Shen Nung, the people lay down peaceful and easy, woke up wide-eyed and blank. They knew their mothers but not their fathers, and lived side by side with the elk and the deer. They plowed for their food, wove for their clothing, and had no thought in their hearts of harming one another. This was Perfect Virtue at its height![5]

Don't get Robber Chih wrong, he doesn't have a primitivist view of families and is not against them per se. Instead, what Chuang-tzu is using Robber Chih to highlight is that the foundation of the family was the root of all social order and systems of government, cultural beliefs, and so on. Hence, Confucianism is judged as natural because it is built on the nucleus of the family. Confucianism is not alone here; many large-scale societies were built on the template of the family. However, that doesn't make any of these societies natural.

The nucleus of the family is an inherently constituted process of human sentient life, and Taoism doesn't deny that. Actually, in pre-Confucian times there were obviously still families within the natural Taoist lifestyle. But for an untrained mind to read Taoist texts too literally with no understanding of metaphor and the general spirit of Chuang-tzu, then they will believe Taoism promotes a primitivist lifestyle. Taoism surely doesn't, and this is a massive problem for any ancient text interpreted in the modern day by those who are metaphorically and symbolically illiterate.

In reality, Taoism is pointing to an intrinsic way of harmony with everything and everyone else, with no need of an overarching external system. For this reason, Robber Chih is the antithesis of Confucian morality and role designation. Chuang-tzu intentionally sets up Robber Chih as the rough carnivalesque counter image to the meek and hypocritical moralist Confucius. Everything about Robber Chih distorts the Confucian regime of sincerity and overidentification with roles. His comical nature is rooted in the dissonance between his name and form. For example, Robber Chih is healthy, handsome, intelligent, charismatic, and yet his form is contradicted by the depreciative role designation of "robber."

These contradictory mismatches between actuality and social representation reoccur all throughout the story. Such contradictions don't sit well with Confucius. They go against his whole worldview of a congruity between name and form. As a result, Confucius has a tactic in the story to praise Robber Chih for his appearance and character but wants him to replace his name of "robber" with an aristocratic title. The title of "robber" conflicts with Confucius's worldview. Upon hearing Confucius's plea, Robber Chih is infuriated. Robber Chih then proceeds to ridicule Confucius in one of the intellectual beatdowns of the ages. At the beginning, Robber Chih explains his appearance and character while alluding to the inherent hypocrisy of Confucius:

> Ch'iu [Confucius], come forward! Those who can be swayed with offers of gain or reformed by a babble of words are mere idiots, simpletons, the commonest sort of men! The fact that I am big and tall, and so handsome that everyone delights to look at me—this is a virtue inherited from my father and mother. Even without your praises, do you think I would be unaware of it? Moreover, I have heard that those who are fond of praising men to their faces are also fond of damning them behind their backs.[6]

The incongruity informing the paradoxical humor in the Robber Chih story, along with the social critique narrative, is that between name and form. The correspondence between the name and form of many of the characters in the story is undermined. The decisive difference between the opposing worldviews of Confucius and Robber Chih is that the former responds to this incongruity with his standard "rectification of names" philosophy known in Chinese as *zhengming* (正名: Wade-Giles *cheng-ming*; Pinyin *zhengming*). Confucius wants to confirm his so-called noble name by being noble, and he wants Robber Chih to do the same by copying his attitude. Obviously, Robber Chih was completely opposed to the idea of the rectification of names.

The verbal beatdown Robber Chih gave Confucius illustrates the personal and social insanity of the Confucian congruity ideal. Chuang-tzu portrays Robber Chih as the living proof of an opposition against the personal verification of social roles. Robber Chih essentially subverts Confucian morality. But, keep in mind, he is not offering a solution to the insanity socialization produces. He has no desire to set things right by demanding true sincerity instead of hypocrisy. If he had such a desire then he would fall into the same trap as Confucius, because Confucius still had his own personal agenda for the world.

As a result, Robber Chih represents a mismatch between name and form, and he does not strive to correct it. Rather, he thrives and lives happily as a deviant outside the law. He plays the role of robber with expert skill, but he is not internally a robber. Thus, he does not verify the name "robber" with his innate being. That is precisely why he couldn't care less about Confucius's proposition to change his name to an aristocratic title. Robber Chih best symbolizes Chuang-tzu's zero perspective—no name or form could define the Tao coursing through all of our veins from the infinite still-point within the center of everything. Hence, Robber

Chih reminded Confucius that instead of focusing on his outward appearance as a robber, maybe Confucius should try and understand why his own philosophy is destroying our nature: "There's no robber worse than you. Why doesn't the world call you Robber Confucius instead of calling me Robber Zhi [Chih]?"[7]

In the end of the story, Robber Chih has had enough and tells Confucius to leave immediately. Confucius is completely flustered after Robber Chih's truth serum. When Confucius goes to grab the reins of his carriage, he fumbles them three times, and his eyes are blank and unseeing, while his face is the color of dead ashes. This representation of Confucius illustrates his lack of genuineness because his fake role of this pious, noble individual was exposed for being false and hypocritical.

Chih's whole function through parody in the text is to expose our own falseness and hypocrisy of the roles and individuals we fool ourselves into believing we are. Robber Chih, then, ultimately represents the unconditioned naturalness within all of us that has no name or form, and this essentially is the essence of Taoist philosophy. But Taoism is not completely against social roles and certain responsibilities attached to those roles. Taoism acknowledges that playing roles is an existential condition of social life. There is no way around it. The problem is this condition is realized by few, as most of us continue to mindlessly move to the beat of a drum based on an image we've created for ourselves. The few who realize this existential condition, on the other hand, are who we refer to as a genuine, authentic, perfected person and true human of Tao, and ultimately, what we know as the great Taoist sage.

THE REBELLION OF THE TAOIST SAGE

The origins of the genuineness of the Taoist sage, a.k.a. genuine person, are discovered first in the Tao Te Ching. In the text there is the Chinese word *zhen* (真: Wade-Giles *chen*; Pinyin *zhen*), which means "having variation and being genuine." This is the authenticity at the core of our being that has no relation to our persona; it is something much deeper. Zhen, then, is elaborated further in the Chuang-tzu text where we first discover the Chinese word *zhenren* (真人: Wade-Giles *chen-jen*; Pinyin *zhenren*), or "genuine person," essentially the nature of the Taoist sage. Basically, a zhenren is somebody who embodies genuineness and, in doing so, has become an aperture for the Tao to express itself.

The appearance of a zhenren in society is a disaster for any established social system or ideology. Having variation, the zhenren can move through life like a butterfly and not be stuck to any position they may have; nor are they stuck in their mind. They are completely free from any illusionary boundary. This all begins with the most deceptive boundary, one's self-image due to one's social role. A zhenren, or "genuine person," is capable of not internalizing any roles, which runs counter to Confucianism and the regime of sincerity. Their social roles can almost never touch them inwardly. For this reason, they enact roles playfully and skillfully. The big difference between a zhenren and us mere mortals is they don't identify with any role. As a result, Hans-Georg Moeller and Paul D'Ambrosio suggest that we could call a zhenren a "genuine pretender" and their unidentified actions as "genuine pretending."

Genuine pretending essentially means that you understand that any role you have is *played*. We cannot but play roles in a social environment, which also stands true for simple communities that existed before Confucianism. But the important word for a Taoist in regard to roles is *played*. You play your role well, but the role can never define who you honestly are. It is just something you are doing temporarily because you have variation and move with the river of Tao.

A zhenren, or genuine pretender if you will, understands there is no correspondence between our role and our natural essence. No falseness or hypocrisy is involved with this state because there is no contradiction between an authentic self and an inauthentic role player. A zhenren, or a Taoist sage in general, enacts roles knowing they are temporary and coincidental. So a Taoist can change roles without taking them seriously or allowing them to become embodied. That Taoist moves through life without being attached to anything, especially not to the parts they play. The condition of being human is we play roles, but we must thoroughly understand that all roles are being played.

A zhenren can assume any appearance in life without suffering because they reside in the still point of the Tao, the zero perspective where the game of "this" and "that" has dissolved (more on that later). But how can we experience that? How do we unravel ourselves from the socialization we've all endured to become a zhenren? To do so, we have to relearn the natural template for being human. The natural Taoist way is so radically opposed to the socialization we've endured that many find it hard to embody after years of conditioning. A Taoist sage allows their genuineness to flow because they have deprogramed themselves from the tyranny of socialization. And sagehood awaits all of us who are willing to accept Taoism as it is. It essentially is a technology for those interested in true liberation, the liberation from one's accumulative identity.

3

The Dissolution
of Identity

To be free in this life, we must unlearn what we've gained and relearn what we've lost. What you will read about in the following chapters is a relearning of the natural way that has been eclipsed by what we've gained, the process of socialization. Then, and only then, will we become a bona fide zhenren. This means, though, that we have to examine and dismantle our identity as it is the byproduct of socialization. This is one of the most uncomfortable processes, but a necessary evil on the spiritual path, especially in Taoism.

One of the common misconceptions of Taoism in the West is that it is a path solely focused on flow and the art of living without any need for getting our hands dirty. This view is a very airy-fairy perspective of Taoism. It excludes the very thing that needs to dissolve to be in flow and embody the art of living—identity. With a strong sense of identity, none of the Taoist principles can be lived.

Some of these inane views of Taoism come from incorrect translations and other translations with no explanation. For example, someone will read in the Tao Te Ching about unlearning and think it is about unlearning what they've learned, such as education, and also couple that with an unlearning of trying to know the Tao. And both may be necessary, and in part true, but they are not the whole puzzle. What unlearning really means in the Tao Te Ching is the unlearning of our identity, that thing within us that is the accumulative product of socialization. As discussed in previous chapters, the identity or ego acts as a fundamental blockage to the fundamental forces and flow of Tao.

The fear people have concerning the dissolution of identity is that they incorrectly believe they won't function without an identity, as if there is nothing intrinsically there without the ego. This is simply not true and something you will learn later in this book. People in the modern world, and especially Westerners, are often more favorable toward Taoism and Yoga, but they are more suspicious of Advaita Vedanta and Buddhism because of the inaccurate belief that the underlying premise of the dissolution of self of the latter two traditions doesn't exist in the former two. This is simply untrue.

To be sure, the dissolution of the ego, self, or identity is the common principle and goal of many Eastern spiritual traditions. The methods and philosophy to achieve that end are different among the traditions and explained differently, but the principle is the same. Achieving such a dissolution is referred to in Hinduism and Buddhism as enlightenment but worded differently when referring to the sage in Taoism, as we discover with the word *zhenren*. Nevertheless, there is a natural state of being that we fundamentally are but has been suppressed. Essentially, we are all inherently enlightened but we've forgotten and must unlearn to realize this truth.

This fundamental truth of innate enlightenment within the Eastern spiritual traditions I sum up with one phrase: *Enlightenment is the dissolution of "I" and the reidentification with the ultimate reality.* The ultimate reality, as discussed, is known as either Brahman in Advaita Vedanta or Tao in Taoism. The reidentification with the ultimate reality in Advaita Vedanta is known as the realization that Atman (undifferentiated consciousness) within all *is* Brahman. You are one with Brahman as Brahman. Likewise, in Taoism, reidentification is the result of letting go of identity and merging as one with the river of Tao. To merge with the river of Tao requires a complete dissolution of identity.

To express our inherent virtue (te) according to our unique organic pattern (li), we must stop fighting the world according to our identity and let go of it so that the river's power can become our power. We fight the current of the river of Tao because we see the world through the veil of identity. We measure the reality according to our identity and incorrectly believe that's the way the world is. It is not. It is only the way our identity perceives it, and then all sorts of narratives are created, leading to conflict and confusion. Paradoxically, if we are serious about world peace, then the one who yearns for peace must disappear. World peace can never be attainable through personas created by the socialization process.

So the conflict we are constantly trying to resolve can never be rectified if the solution is filtered through identity, which is inherently flawed by self-interest and conditioning. Our innate nature knows no form of conflict because it is naturally harmonious and one with the river. Our nature was warped due to socialization and, as a result, the accumulation of a separate isolated self was born. The destruction of our nature is nothing new. Since the birth of agrarian cultures and large-scale societies, our nature has been distorted. Chuang-tzu warned us about socialization almost twenty-five hundred years ago due to the increasing tyranny of Confucianism.

THE STORY OF HUNDUN

In the very last part of the inner chapters of the Chuang-tzu text, there is an extremely important story that encapsulates the whole Taoist philosophy and view of identity and social conditioning. This is the story of *Hundun* (混沌: Wade-Giles *Hun-tun*; Pinyin *Hundun*). The word *Hundun* is known in its Cantonese variation as *Wonton*, a famous mixed dumpling that you may have eaten. But Hundun in the Chuang-tzu is no mixed dumpling; it is some primordial state before the world of forms came into manifestation.

In ancient China, Hundun is a type of mythological being that represents the original state of the universe. Hundun is an indistinct primordial being without any features or qualities, similar to the Greek notion of *chaos*, the qualityless state of Nirguna Brahman in Advaita Vedanta, and the original state of Tao in wu chi. Hundun—as with chaos, Nirguna Brahman, and wu chi—is the cosmogenic idea that the universe emerges from an undifferentiated embryonic wholeness, rather than a divine being or creator God. This is similar among many Eastern spiritual traditions, as we discover with the undifferentiated and ultimate reality of Brahman in Sanatana Dharma (Hinduism). The idea of the undifferentiated whole in ancient China is not only found in the Chuang-tzu, it is also prevalent in the Tao Te Ching and the Huai-nan-tzu (淮南子: Wade-Giles *Huai-nan-tzu*; Pinyin *Huainanzi*), another ancient Chinese text. The undifferentiated whole of Hundun is a great oneness, an ultimate state of simplicity where there is only peace and equanimity. Hundun is a state of balance where the world of flux has not eventuated, at least not yet.

In the story this state of balance and great wholeness and oneness is disturbed by two emperors who seek to change Hundun's nature. This is where the story has a deeply significant meaning for how we too are changed by the world around us. The story states:

The emperor of the South Sea was called Shu [Brief], the emperor of the North Sea was called Hu [Sudden], and the emperor of the central region was called Hun-tun [Chaos]. Shu and Hu from time to time came together for a meeting in the territory of Hun-tun, and Hun-tun treated them very generously. Shu and Hu discussed how they could repay his kindness. "All men," they said, "have seven openings so they can see, hear, eat, and breathe. But Hun-tun alone doesn't have any. Let's trying boring him some!"

Every day they bored another hole, and on the seventh day Hun-tun died.[1]

The death of Hundun after seven holes were bored into him by Shu and Hu is very significant to our plight as individuals, which will make more sense as we dissect this passage. There are a few ways to understand this story that actually all relate to each other. For this reason, I will merge them together to give you a greater understanding.

In the great wholeness of Hundun, all life energies are unspent. Hundun's potentiality is infinite, and its tranquility unencumbered. But once Shu and Hu bore seven holes into Hundun, he becomes a distinct human being. His unspent life energies leak out. These facial openings of the senses slowly but surely drain human vitality and eventually kill us, especially if they are overstimulated. This is a common theme in the Chuang-tzu, as we discover with the *fasting the mind* passage. The nature of any large-scale society is extremely busy, and we give away our simplicity to keep up with the Joneses. Stress, anxiety, depression, suicide, and, essentially, a short life is the result.

The Taoist longevity model is based on simplicity and an eradication of the social habits that make us busy. Just like Hundun, we innocently allow society to drain our energy without any resistance. Day by day our vital energies are depleted because our facial holes or senses are constantly leaking. The Tao Te Ching warns us about our energies draining, but it also offers us a solution if we are serious about our health and sanity:

> *Fill the openings, close the entries—be*
> *unencumbered by the termination of the*
> *body. Open the openings, be busy with*
> *affairs—and you will not be saved from*
> *the termination of the body.[2]*

Filling the openings and closing the entries symbolizes a return to the formless whole nature of Hundun. This life practice of returning to our wholeness or oneness is to harness our vitality, which requires us to embrace simplicity. In Yogic philosophy there is the fifth limb of the eight-limb system (Ashtanga Yoga), which is known in Sanskrit as *Pratyahara*, meaning "withdrawal of the senses." Pratyahara allows the yogi to remain in their original state without their senses being drawn here and there due to the gravitational pull of the external world. A yogi knows their Hundun nature very well. Likewise, the ancient Taoists practiced the same withdrawal by disentangling their awareness and senses from the external world.

We, too, have to engage in the same process if we are to reclaim our health and sanity. Our senses must not succumb to the temptations of socialization and the busyness it produces. The more we obediently follow the external world, the more we define ourselves as an identity. Essentially, our vitality leaks out when we continue this ongoing process of accumulating an identity. By defining yourself, as Hundun did, you are killing your nature slowly. But just like

Hundun, we are none the wiser. We follow socialization without question. But, in the end, the longevity interpretation of Hundun opens the door to a deeper cause and somewhat the root of social busyness itself.

HUNDUN'S WARNING
OF CONFORMITY

Socialization itself drives busyness and, according to the story, is the underlying motive behind Shu and Hu's eagerness to drill holes into Hundun's face. Busyness, then, is driven by the beliefs a society values. These beliefs can be due to a culture, political orientation, religion, or any type of ideology. But in the end, it is all conditioning trying to make our original nature "natural" through an artificial process (like with Confucianism in the previous chapter). This unnatural process is enhanced by enacting roles according to the regime of sincerity championed by Confucius.

Acting according to our social roles and statuses depletes our vitality because, according to the Hundun analogy, our openings are leaking profusely. So socialization itself is what affects our longevity and solidifies our identity, which is the deeper meaning of the story. Hundun himself represents Chuang-tzu's zero perspective, where no role or distinction could ever exist. Hundun is serene and peaceful. Enter Shu and Hu, the champions of socialization in the Warring States form of Confucianism. Shu and Hu represent the mainstream conventions of the time. It pains them to see Hundun not defined, not cultured. They cannot understand his state, so they want to establish a bond with him by spreading the word of socialization, similar to the way Jehovah's Witnesses go door-to-door seeking to influence you with their own version of reality.

Shu and Hu essentially want to shape Hundun in their own image by drilling him a face. The evolutionary strategy of groups, from small-scale to large-scale, has been about shaping others in the image of what the group accepts. To be Taoist, on the other hand, is akin to being an outlaw. This attitude makes the so-called cultured people uncomfortable, and so they are eager to change anyone who doesn't fall in line with their beliefs.

We also try to shape people on an individual level, as most people unconsciously, or sometimes consciously, try to mold others and even the world in their own self-image. It gives us the illusion of security because we feel we have teammates who will protect our separatist views and beliefs. In the same vein, Shu and Hu want Hundun to conform so that they can share the same form with Hundun. Shu and Hu, who represent mainstream convention, intend to civilize all those who look and think differently and are not part of the conventional sociopolitical order, in this case, Confucianism.

The story is a timeless warning that any society, culture, or ideology has a political desire to shape what or whoever is different from them according to their own image. This political desire, as we all surely know, informs many conflicts and wars. The Hundun story, then, is in part a critique of interventionist politics that meddle heavily with people and nature, which is diametrically opposed to Taoism's essential teaching of wu-wei, noninterference. Even the editor of the Chuang-tzu, Guo Xiang, in the fourth century, stated that Shu and Hu destroyed Hundun with their activist interference. Taoism itself is a critique of interference in general, and Hundun represents the danger for anyone who internalizes and conforms to the machinations of socialization.

THE FAILED TAOIST SAGE

At the end of the story, Hundun dies. Why? Shu and Hu's so-called noble intentions are misguided and their course of action inept. They try to shape Hundun in their own image, and they kill him.

Shu and Hu are not wise sages or rulers after all, but rather damn fools who are the puppets of interventionist politics. They failed Hundun because they fell for the "naturalize what is not natural" model proposed by Confucius. Hundun was completely whole and at peace until the socialization police came knocking. Hundun could not thwart their actions, and so he represents a failed Taoist sage just like the failures of Shu and Hu.

There is no real winner in this story. Hundun is a failure because he cluelessly submitted to the psychological conditioning of socialization. He lacked a strategy of evasion and could not conserve his natural simplicity. He conformed without question. Hundun allowed Shu and Hu to mutilate his nature, which killed him. The reason Hundun died is because the process of social indoctrination kills your true nature, shaping you to whatever the overarching ideology dictates. We have all gone through this type of death naively.

We fail ourselves when we allow socialization to shape us. We willingly accept the false myths that indoctrinate people, which then create illusionary knowledge and give false authority and power to those who spread such unreliable wisdom. Once we believe in the powerful but often hollow mythologies of any time, when we embrace the ideologies and false narratives they entail, and when we internalize the moral norms they impose on people, we allow the process of socialization to drill holes into our faces so that we adopt an artificial identity.

We all resemble Hundun still to this day when we uncritically identify with the ideological conditioning drilled into us by the dubious authorities who surround us. We accept the rule of authority in many guises. We don't question and instead accept the way it is, or I should say, the way we think it is—the way of the Tao is the way it truly is. When we accept the ideologies and narrative of our time, we die just like Hundun. We crucify ourselves to an artificial dogma to suit the society and culture to which we believe we belong. But the story of Hundun's death ridicules and deflates grand narratives of any age proposed by any world view. Taoism has no grand truth claim or universal knowledge of a creator God. Rather, it is based on the way of nature, the way of the Tao.

From the still point of the Tao, the zero perspective, all grand narratives and ideologies are mere constructs of language and employed politically to mold people in the image of the magical wordplay of an ideology. We want to bend nature to suit our view of life. Our eagerness to build the world in our image reveals an underlying psychopathy within human beings.

THE ANTHROPOCENTRIC ILLUSION

Hundun is the center of the world, the undifferentiated original state of the cosmos. As Chuang-tzu said, "the still-point of the Tao where one can see the infinite in the ten thousand things." But the center of the world is under constant pressure from the paragons of duality seeking to warp its whole nature. In the story, Shu and Hu want to humanize the center of the world, Hundun. They do this because of an underlying bias and illusion most human beings share, the idea that humans are the center of the world. Many religions fervently promote and share this human-centric view. We measure all life based on this anthropocentric view.

People tend to fall for this illusion unconsciously. It is promoted extensively by some religions who have a vested interest in our acquiescence. Christianity, for example, will put human beings on a pedestal and have an indifferent view of everything else in nature because, well, Jesus was a man who was the son of God/is God and he is the "only" way, as most Christians politically state to gain new followers. As a result, especially in the West, since the cognitive style is fashioned after Christianity, we believe humans are special. All sorts of pathologies and insensitivity toward nature occur after we embody anthropocentrism. As a result, everything nonhuman is made to fit human society and its standards and values until, eventually, anything nonhuman becomes extinct. Prolific writer and philosopher Aldous Huxley elaborates on this human-centric view in relation to the story of Hundun:

> In this delicately comic parable Chaos is Nature in the state of *wu-wei*—non-assertion or equilibrium. Shu and Hu are the living images of those busy persons who thought they would improve on Nature by turning dry prairies into wheat fields, and produced deserts; who proudly proclaimed the Conquest of the Air, and then discovered that they had defeated civilization; who chopped down vast forests to provide the newsprint demanded by that universal literacy which was to make the world safe for intelligence and democracy, and got wholesale erosion, pulp magazines and the organs of Fascist, Communist, capitalist and nationalist propaganda. In brief, Shu and Hu are devotees of the apocalyptic religion of Inevitable Progress, and their creed is that the Kingdom of Heaven is outside you, and in the future. Chuang Tzu, on the other hand, like all good Taoists, has no desire to bully Nature into subserving ill-considered temporal ends, at variance with the final end of men as formulated in the Perennial Philosophy. His wish is to work with Nature, so as to produce material and social conditions in which individuals may realize Tao on every level from the psychological up to the spiritual.[3]

We are all slowly being brainwashed by the apocalyptic religion of "Inevitable Progress," as Huxley put it. All governments and nations are clamoring over each other in this game. Most human beings are completely severed from everything else in this world. They have no real relationship with nature other than how it can serve us and appease our material needs. One might go for a hike to try and reconnect with nature, and this is great, but frankly minor in an attempt to reconnect. Again, this follows the notion that we want something from nature rather than living as one with it. *Nature must serve us and facilitate social human progress* is the underlying mantra. We are the center of the world after all, right? This domineering attitude, whether we want to admit it or not, is a Western cognitive temperament stemming from individualism, which is in part based on Christianity. As Huxley explains:

> Compared with that of the Taoists and Far Eastern Buddhists, the Christian attitude towards Nature has been curiously insensitive and often downright domineering and violent. Taking their cue from an unfortunate remark in Genesis, Catholic moralists have regarded animals as mere things which men do right to exploit for their own ends. Like landscape painting, the humanitarian movement in Europe was an almost completely secular affair. In the Far East both were essentially religious.[4]

Our individualistic mentality is destroying nature because individualism itself is inherently self-interested. The more we think of ourselves on a personal level, the less we sympathize with everything else. *My* life must be taken care of, *my* needs are what is important. And, sure, our lives do have needs, and they should be taken care of, but not with an individualistic, human-centric perspective. If we knew we weren't special but understood we were a part of a greater whole, then we'd do our best to live harmoniously with the world and other people. But individualism cons us into thinking we are special, that we are unique.

Hearing that we are special our whole life, from our parents to the collective culture, fools us into thinking we actually are. We're not. We are only special in the sense that we are part of something much greater than ourselves, and yet we cannot live in harmony with it. We destroy nature to meet our artificial needs. These artificial needs are not only destroying nature but driving us mad. We'll do anything to be famous, to gain attention, to be unparalleled, even at the expense of our mental health.

Imagine how many resources would be saved if society didn't create artificial needs within us and if we didn't fall for those ideas? There would be a drastic decrease in resource consumption, and, collectively, we could regain our health and sanity. But we've come so far that we are starting to believe we will exhaust our resources on Earth, and so we are exploring the potential of space travel to colonize another planet, essentially establishing another ideology stemming from oversensationalized mass media, corporations, and influential people for their own covert reasons. Mars is the next frontier for us to plunder resources to maintain our unnatural way of life. Instead of examining the artificial needs of society that waste so many resources, we want to leave this planet to maintain these artificial needs that we have become habituated to. We could simply change our habits, but the economic machine won't allow that.

Why stop "Inevitable Progress" when we can just bounce from one planet to the next plundering their resources? We can keep fooling ourselves into thinking that progress and the demands it requires are healthy and sane for us long-term. We have to come to our senses to realize that human beings aren't the pinnacle of nature's creations. Individually, none of us are special. Now this may seem like a depressing view of ourselves, but actually it liberates us from the constant pressure of trying to be special and unique. Remember, society has fooled us into believing that our worth is measured by how much attention we can garner. Being rich and famous is not all it's cracked up to be. There's no need to win the rat race or beat the Joneses. It's all an illusion, propaganda. It's all baloney!

You don't have to try to belong. You already belong to the universe, to the Tao, but as one with all life. You are not alone out there, which is a common anxiety produced by individualism. You are always one with the Tao. The problem is we've cut ourselves off from the Tao because the chase and the hunt have maddened our hearts, to paraphrase Lao-tzu. We fight the river because we are under the illusion that we are special and at odds with the river, different than it. We believe we are above all other life forms and so they serve our needs because they exist *for* us. Taoist philosophy subverts this type of thinking.

In Taoism, we are constantly humbling ourselves with the cold hard facts of reality. For example, it's common for a Taoist to acknowledge that a human is no more special than an ant. We really find that hard to believe, but that's a fact. An ant and a human are one, neither more special or more necessary than the other. The Earth is not here to serve us; we are a small part of the ecosystem of the planet, and we make up a harmonious aspect of nature, but in no way do we have dominion over anything else. We essentially serve the planet, not vice versa. We are equal with all other organisms, and we make up a unified whole that the Tao flows through.

Socialization drills holes into our face. Eventually, we take the drill from society's hands and begin to drill holes into our own faces as we continually reinforce our indoctrination. We feel safe within the conditioning we've endured. As a result, we essentially build our own anthropocentric universe where we feel special and unique on an individual level. But our personal views aren't special or unique. They are built on the foundation of socialization, and so our personal views aren't essentially even our own or isolated to us. Our separate isolated identity is not the center of the universe or special in anyway. Socialization and the resulting identity are an impediment to the natural process of the world. A kind of interference that disturbs the natural flow of the river of Tao. Our identity is a blockage from receiving the fundamental forces of Tao. The story of Hundun is the story of ourselves, a double-edged sword of life when we walk away from our divinity to take on an isolated identity.

IN HUNDUN'S IMAGE

We are all the center of the world as Hundun, mythological beings representing the original state of the universe, not as humans. The process of our lives is the same initiation process Hundun had to go through at the hands of Shu and Hu. From birth we are pure, innocent, and have a mind that is free to explore life with no filters hindering the experience. But socialization begins at a young age. We are constantly informed about how to behave and what is acceptable according to the culture we are raised in. This whole process is achieved unconsciously by our parents and then intentionally by education, as one must learn to serve the machine without question.

Society, culture, religion, education, and our family, to varying degrees, contort our nature. Don't get me wrong, as a parent you surely do have a responsibility to guide your children and equip them with some knowledge about life and the world. But there is a limit to how much a child needs to know without interfering too much with their nature. The more we go through this process of socialization, we die just like Hundun. But our death, due to this process, is a psychological and spiritual death. As Brad Pitt's character Tyler Durden poignantly explains in the film *Fight Club*:

Man, I see in Fight Club the strongest and smartest men who've ever lived. I see all this potential, and I see it squandered. God damn it, an entire generation pumping gas, waiting tables—slaves with white collars. Advertising has us chasing cars and clothes, working jobs we hate so we can buy shit we don't need. We're the middle children of history, man. No purpose or place. We have no Great War. No Great Depression. Our great war is a spiritual war. Our great depression is our lives. We've all been raised on television to believe that one day we'd all be millionaires, and movie gods, and rock stars, but we won't. And we're slowly learning that fact. And we're very, very pissed off.[5]

Just like Hundun, we cluelessly submit to society. As a result, we die little by little every day, as the world constantly tells us how we ought to be rather than allowing us to be as we are. Pop culture, for example, makes millions of young and impressionable people do things they wouldn't ordinarily do. They may begin to act and dress a certain way because a pop singer may dress this way, or they might have a distorted view of the world because an influential athlete does.

We become a caricature of what culture shoves in our faces. For example, one idol has pink hair and tattoos from neck to toe and millions blindly follow suit. We are being played. In such a world heavily influenced by pop culture, it is hard for many people, especially the youth, to be genuine and authentic. But we must have the awareness to identify an artificial culture that seeks to shape us to become puppets for corporations to use as they see fit. As ethnobotanist and psychonaut Terence McKenna is known to have once said, "Culture is not your friend." When we unknowingly believe culture is our friend, we die little by little every day until our original Hundun nature is unrecognizable.

We were once wholly complete and one with the Tao until the world changed us. Essentially, we are all divine like Hundun until we are made human. Human in this sense is the confused cultural creature we all know too well, the socialized beast. Socialization molds our pure nature to the point that we embody an artificial identity that we live through until we believe the world revolves around us. It's similar to how people used to think the Earth was the center of the universe until Nicolaus Copernicus brought the truth to the fore to dispel our illusion. Likewise, Lao-tzu and Chuang-tzu (and Eastern spirituality in general) dispels the illusion that our egos and identities are the center of the world. Actually, they take it a step further by revealing that our identities don't really exist and are not essentially who we are.

Subtract socialization and its subsequent identity, and we are back in Hundun's image, the image of the being that represents the original state of the universe—nature in its purest form. We are a representation of Hundun. We are all a localization of the *one consciousness*.

Many Eastern spiritual traditions verify this experience of ego or identity dissolution to reveal the true underlying ultimate reality. What inhibits this realization is that we identify with the equipment on the localized level, meaning the body, mind, and essentially the accumulative sense of self, identity, and ego. We believe we are the equipment rather than the source. Our lives are invested in the equipment that fools us into believing this is who we are. Our movement is in the outward trajectory, moving us far away from the source. Socialization drills holes into our faces so that we serve its ends rather than realizing our true nature, and we continue that work because we want to continually define ourselves to stick out from others. This is true mindlessness. We must return to our original Hundun nature or else we will continue to die spiritually and psychologically in life. We must know our original face before the human world bored holes into it.

YOUR ORIGINAL FACE

Zen Buddhism speaks of your *original face* before you were born. Advaita Vedanta speaks of the undifferentiated consciousness of Atman that is the *ultimate reality* of Brahman. Yoga speaks of the *pure awareness* of Purusha, which is separate from the phenomenal world, Prakriti. And Taoism speaks of the same philosophy in the Tao Te Ching and Chuang-tzu texts, especially through stories such as Hundun, not to mention the constant reference to the zhenren, the "genuine person."

In most Eastern spiritual traditions, the original face or undifferentiated consciousness principle is a foundation of the philosophies. As a result, all of our awareness training is to return to our original faces. The reverse of the t'ai chi trajectory is to abide in your true nature, your original face. Why Hundun is a failed Taoist sage is because he unknowingly allowed his awareness to be dragged into the complex process of socialization. And yet, just like Hundun, we have all endured this process as well.

Our pure awareness was hijacked and intermingled with the complexity of the world. To avoid this ongoing enchantment, we must reclaim our awareness so that we can be natural again. Being as nature intended is the most difficult process we can go through (as we will discover in the following chapters). We must fill in the holes the world has bored into our faces, as the Tao Te Ching put it. To fill in those holes, our motion of awareness must move from our identity to the nature of the Tao, the stillness of wu chi, as explained by the reversal of the trajectory described in previous chapters.

Chuang-tzu's spiritual practice to counter socialization's drill is a method known as *fasting the mind*. One of my previous books is dedicated to this practice, aptly titled *Fasting the Mind*. Actually, this practice, also called *mind fasting*, is not isolated to Chuang-tzu, even though the term comes directly from the Chuang-tzu text when translated into English. Fasting the mind is spread across ancient Eastern philosophy, including the Advaita Vedanta tradition in Hinduism, the practice of Vipassana in Theravada Buddhism, open-awareness meditation in Zen Buddhism, and Dzogchen in Vajrayana Buddhism.

However, it is in the Chuang-tzu text that the practice takes shape. In the fasting the mind passage, Confucius as the master and Yen Hui as the student are in dialogue about a corrupt ruler in the state of Wei. Usually Chuang-tzu does not have a favorable view of Confucius's philosophy, as we see vividly in the Robber Chih passage. But in this passage Confucius plays the mouthpiece of Chuang-tzu because Confucius was the most popular philosopher during that period in China. In this particular passage, Yen Hui has devised many schemes to try to make the ruler of Wei benevolent and compassionate toward his people, whom he has neglected for far too long. But Confucius is not at all convinced by his plans. He feels that Yen Hui is trying to influence the ruler with his own beliefs. After shooting down many hatched schemes, Confucius has had enough and explains to Yen Hui:

> Confucius said, "Goodness, how could that do? You have too many policies and plans and you haven't seen what is needed. You will probably get off without incurring any blame, yes. But that will be as far as it goes. How do you think you can actually convert him? You are still making the mind your teacher!"
>
> Yen Hui said, "I have nothing more to offer. May I ask the proper way?"
>
> "You must fast!" said Confucius. "I will tell you what that means. Do you think it

is easy to do anything while you have [a mind]? If you do, Bright Heaven will not sanction you."

Yen Hui said, "My family is poor. I haven't drunk wine or eaten any strong foods for several months. So can I be considered as having fasted?"

"That is the fasting one does before a sacrifice, not the fasting of the mind."

"May I ask what the fasting of the mind is?"

Confucius said, "Make your will one! Don't listen with your ears, listen with your mind. No, don't listen with your mind, but listen with your spirit. Listening stops with the ears, the mind stops with recognition, but spirit is empty and waits on all things. The Way gathers in emptiness alone. Emptiness is the fasting of the mind."

Yen Hui said, "Before I heard this, I was certain that I was Hui. But now that I have heard it, there is no more Hui. Can this be called emptiness?"

"That's all there is to it," said Confucius. "Now I will tell you. You may go and play in his bird cage, but never be moved by fame. If he listens, then sing; if not, keep still. Have no gate, no opening, but make oneness your house and live with what cannot be avoided. Then you will be close to success."[6]

There are many similarities between this passage and Hundun's. Confucius explains to Yen Hui that he should have no opening and make oneness his house. These openings are filled by fasting the mind, by listening with the spiritual essence of emptiness. Confucius explains to Yen Hui that the Tao gravitates toward and gathers in emptiness alone, which is a reference also to the bellows and valley spirit found in the Tao Te Ching.

Just like the bellows and valley spirit, our fundamental nature is empty, which is described in Buddhism with the Sanskrit word *Sunyata*. It is socialization that colors consciousness, giving us definition. To fast the mind from the socialization process, we must guard our senses and not allow the subjective views, beliefs, and agendas of any false authority to enter through our eyes or ears. We must protect ourselves from being shaped by the world. One must reverse the trajectory of awareness to keep the mind empty and pristine.

By fasting the mind, we fill in the holes bored into our faces by society. We must reign in our socialized awareness training that has mixed our senses with the external world and instead withdraw our senses and turn within. This withdrawal will fill in the holes and return our minds to equanimity. In practicing mind fasting, we return to our original faces. Yen Hui had to come back to his original face, devoid of identity. All of his plans, schemes, beliefs, and personal agendas are from his conditioned identity, which can only cause more conflict and confusion.

We can never solve a problem with more problems, and that's what we are constantly doing in the world. Chuang-tzu's point in the passage is that only from your original face can life be lived fully and our actions and reactions be emotionally clean and spontaneous. Yen Hui had to act from his original face and from there, as the Tao Te Ching is known to state, "When nothing is done, nothing is left undone." But just like Yen Hui, we have to realize that the way we act and react are based on the indoctrination we've endured.

Your actions, reactions, emotions, and behavior are from your conditioned identity that was constructed by socialization. If we live life from this accumulative identity, then our very life is inauthentic.

Because the way we behave is due to the socialization program we have ingested, we do not experience reality from emptiness, but rather through rose-colored glasses. The further our pure awareness moves from the center, the more deluded we will become, and the results of this delusion will be catastrophic. If you are serious about Taoism, or Eastern spirituality in general, then you have to examine why you act and react a certain way according to life. After a thorough examination, you'll discover that your actions and reactions are not authentic.

The story of Hundun is about not allowing the world to cultivate this isolated separate sense of self. Instead we need to come back to our original faces as Yen Hui did. Imagine the world we would live in if we all dissolved this illusory accumulative identity? How would you act and react genuinely from your original state? What would the world look like from your original face? In the following chapters you'll discover how the world honestly is, exactly how nature intended.

4

The Immorality
of Morality

The way the world truly is and the way we think it is according to socialization are light years apart. Case in point is morality. Most people feel morality is just and keeps the balance of society in check. And that may be the case on the surface, but it is very far from the truth.

Morality has become such part and parcel of socialization that we lack the foresight to question it. I've found in my work that even an innocent and lighthearted critique of morality is met by reactive, emotional resistance, rather than consideration or deep thought. Lao-tzu and Chuang-tzu, on the other hand, exposed the inherent flaws in morality. They did this for many reasons, but mainly to highlight the fact that morality is a man-made invention and not the way of nature.

Taoism, then, being the way of nature, is amoral. The very mention that Taoism is amoral makes many people who believe they are Taoist uncomfortable. Following the way of nature is not easy when we realize how deep social indoctrination is embedded in our bones. But if you want to be as nature intended, then morality must be on trial.

MORALITY PRODUCES
ITS OPPOSITE

Lao-tzu and Chuang-tzu challenged the very fabric of morality for good reason. There is a common theme in both the Tao Te Ching and the Chuang-tzu text that trying to impose a man-made morality and saintly righteousness on the people creates its opposite. One example in these texts is that creating a morality against stealing produces thieves. As a result, man-made moral systems try to fabricate an institutionalized goodness on decent, innocent people, often with disastrous outcomes that condition a person to become someone that they are not naturally. No one is born a thief but anyone may become one. We essentially establish a contrived, socially accepted behavioral matrix that attempts to create a world full of saints but in the end confuses the individual more, leading to people and a world lacking natural genuineness and wisdom. As chapter nineteen of the Tao Te Ching states:

> Give up sainthood, renounce wisdom,
> And it will be a hundred times better for
> everyone.
> Give up kindness, renounce morality,
> And people will rediscover filial piety and love.[1]

For Lao-tzu and Chuang-tzu, the target of such criticism was Confucius. The system of Confucianism, as explained in chapter two, is a socialization process where we must try and naturalize that which isn't natural. This is an impossible feat, as both Lao-tzu and Chuang-tzu explain. Nevertheless, Confucian morality still marched on regardless of the Taoist critique of that time. Women's feet were bound, people slept in a certain position to reflect their social role, and so on. Confucius's view of morality meant women were beneath

men and therefore actually had to mold their bone structure, a physical reflection of their societal restrictions. Likewise with the men of
society, Confucius wanted them to adhere to impossible moral standards in the hope of becoming a *junzi*, superior man. And for all
citizens, Confucian morality created an opposite effect leading to all
sorts of psychopathy (discussed in chapter two). In trying to mold
both sexes with an artificial morality, we drove them literally mad.
People forget the way of nature when an artificial morality arises, as
the Tao Te Ching explains:

> *When the great Tao is forgotten,*
> *Kindness and morality arise.[2]*

Kindness, in this sense, is as artificial as morality. It is not something that should be man-made or function according to the rules
and regulations of socialization. Rather, it should be as natural as
other innate virtues such as humility. Kindness is not something
one needs to speak about or contrive to keep up with the moral
norms; it is as natural as opening and closing your hand. Morality
and kindness are insincere when we order them systematically to
the socialization process. Lao-tzu and Chuang-tzu don't create an
alternative system of morality for us to follow. Instead, they just
explain the way nature genuinely is and that to follow nature means
our psychological disposition is fundamentally amoral. Before society began to mold us at a young age according to its morality, our
original faces, just like everything else in nature, were amoral and
naturally virtuous.

We want people to be pious, but we don't grant them the trust
they deserve, and instead the world thrusts commandments upon
them that are supposed to evoke a socially accepted morality.

Socialization can't get out of the illusion that humans are beasts from birth. It seems society will never consider what Taoism revealed: morality itself produces beasts. Imposed morality is not a system that adapts perfectly to all human beings; we all have different aptitudes for different things. This is how nature is. Any system of morality might be uncomfortably tolerated by some but cannot be embodied by all because it is counter to nature, and the nature within humans can be suppressed but never eradicated.

THE EVIL NATURE OF MORALITY

Morality shaping people according to an ideology and socialization process is obviously not isolated to Confucianism. Society, culture, and religion are all eager to superimpose their own version of morality on the masses. This has been especially prevalent in the last few centuries with the world opening up due to ease of travel and communication and, as a result, cultures clashing. As they clash, we see competition between different sets of moral values based on different cultures.

The fact of the matter is when you have morality, it conflicts with another's view of morality, and it actually conflicts with life itself. This is evident in how both Islam and Christianity (through the British Empire) colonized India. India has been oppressed for centuries, first through Middle Eastern colonization, and then European colonization. The Hindus withstood the onslaught by the Moguls only to be invaded by the British and other European nations. Hundreds of years of colonial consciousness clashing with the Bharat civilization and culture have produced the India we know today.

Hinduism, being a peaceful, pluralistic spiritual tradition, and known as the eternal natural way, has absorbed other religions into the fabric of its society no matter how much damage those foreign cultures have done. India has often been a safe haven for other cultures. A case in point is when Jewish people who were exiled from Israel around 70 CE found a new home in Kerala in the south of India. But even though Hinduism withstood the onslaught of the Moguls and the British, colonial consciousness, or *coloniality*, has affected India deeply with many people at odds with their own heritage. Its influence on the masses runs deep. As author and lawyer J. Sai Deepak states, "coloniality was a form of 'inception' performed on the minds of the colonised so that colonialism and colonisation were no more external to their consciousness, but became internal to it."[3]

Westerners are deeply conditioned by Christian morality the same as Far East Asians are with Confucianism. Even Western atheists tend to operate from the Christian moral perspective. The cognitive style of the West has been fundamentally shaped by Christianity, and this same Christian morality came with the British and was superimposed onto the Hindu people of India, which has influenced India from the ground up.

The *Christian* morality is mistakenly believed by many Western minds to be a *universal* morality. Ideas such as secularism and tolerance are forced on other cultures who already have their own set of morals and values. Christianity, through European imperialism, infected other cultures with coloniality to advance its own morality and sense of spirituality. This is a classic case of *demographic swamping*, a tactic that has been essential for the survival of one set of beliefs at the cost of other people's beliefs and ways of life.

Christianity and Islam, in particular, were very clever at how they approached demographic swamping. Within both the Bible and the Quran is a scriptural or doctrinal privilege that neatly divides the world into believers and nonbelievers, sinners if you will. It is with this scriptural privilege that many condemn other cultures for their own evolution and spirituality.

I have witnessed this undermining condemnation firsthand in many Asian countries. One example was when my wife and I were living in Pokhara, Nepal. Pokhara is such a beautiful place, and the Nepali people are amazing. But one day, while walking along the peaceful Phewa Lake in Pokhara, I saw that there were a group of Christians condemning Nepalis for their culture. They were openly undermining the Hindu and Buddhist spiritual traditions of Nepal by "explaining" to the Nepali people that they are going to hell for believing in false gods. This was extremely frustrating and sad to see. What the radicalized mindset of that group of Bible thumping Christians ignores is that Nepal is steeped in an ancient, rich history of spirituality—a living tradition that evolved organically in that region of the world.

As another example of the repercussions of coloniality, many Pacific Island and Latin American nations have a negative view of being colonized by Europeans, but still fervently follow Christianity even though it is part of the colonial consciousness. It is not indigenous to those countries. The indoctrination is so deep that the very mention that Christianity is an intrinsic tool of coloniality is sometimes met with resistance in those countries.

The Hindu and Buddhist path of Nepal, and anywhere else that follows those ancient traditions, doesn't have a scripture of doctrinal privilege for gaining followers; rather they are sincerely concerned about the true liberation of all beings. The Eastern spiritual traditions don't have an expansionist approach. They are older than the Abrahamic religions, and they wisely follow the path of noninterference without any concern for influencing other cultures with their beliefs. The desire to change other people and interfere with existing cultures reflects an insecurity and immaturity in these younger religions.

For any culture to truly reconnect with its roots seemingly requires a deprogramming of colonialism's influence as well as any other unnatural moral codes intrinsic to that culture. That all begins with identifying a set of moral standards that were forced on them.

SIN VS. NATURE

Abrahamic religions force the moral standard that we are uncultured beasts from birth, perpetuated through the illusion of sin. They are based on impossible moral standards to live up to. The life of Jesus Christ, for example, is an unrealistic standard for people to try to emulate.

The piousness of Jesus is inhuman, essentially, a standard no person could live up to. This standard does not take into account our humanity, our natural inclinations that make us human. No matter whether Jesus was a real historical figure or pure mythology, his standard is not of this world and actually undermines and belittles the world.

Whoever is behind the story seems more worried about the control of the masses, which is why numerous scholars believe the Bible is a political doctrine and not spiritual in any way. It is a doctrinal strategy for imposing impossible moral norms and values on the masses. We should be as inhumanely good as Jesus Christ, but as we've witnessed for millennia, no one can adhere to these standards for their entire life because nature is nature. The concept of sin is a man-made construct.

Nature requires us to be natural, to follow our instincts; that is how we evolved. For example, if no one followed their sexual desires and urges, then we wouldn't exist. Thank God for healthy libidos. But certain ideologies, such as Christianity, turn natural inclinations into sin, a human flaw.

Imposing such morality on natural inclinations breeds artificial guilt, a real and dangerous psychopathy that has been part of the collective psyche for far too long (thousands of years in fact). What should be obvious to the masses, but apparently is not, is that the concept of sin does not contribute to the health and sanity of all people. It might be the path for a priest, but not the masses. Too much of Western religious teachings are focused on sin instead of knowledge. And I don't mean the knowledge one learns according to doctrine, but the knowledge of reality and consciousness itself.

So much of the Abrahamic religions are focused on the stories one is told and the morality embedded in the teachings. There is no real focus on actual self-transformation and liberation, which is completely different from the external idea of salvation. Some may argue that the moral norms transform their character, but that is only true to the extent that their transformation is based on the artifice of man-made morals, not based on how nature is. We can't fight nature and think we will win; we are nature. Believing you are a sinner puts you at war with yourself. We surely are not sinners by nature. We are only sinners to the degree that we accept the man-made doctrine that says we are so.

A great example of sin versus nature is sexual orientation. Christianity, for example, inculcates guilt within a homosexual person because the religious teachings make them feel like there is something wrong with them. The truth is there isn't; they are perfect as they are. This is another example of religious morality advising us to suppress our nature. Similar to our discussion of the moral standpoint of not stealing leading to thieves, thousands of years of sexual repression has led to a perverted societal view of sex and sexuality.

This perversion of sex has also distorted many philosophies of the East. The very mention of Tantra to Westerners evokes visions of sexual intercourse, and the sexual alchemy in Taoism is similarly misunderstood and somehow perceived as an essential aspect of the philosophy. Both traditions have been incorrectly related to physical sexual intercourse rather than the alchemical marriage of the masculine and feminine energies of the universe that are within all of us (yang and yin or Shiva and Shakti). It is as if the Western suppression of natural inclinations clouds our perceptions when we are introduced to new ideas and concepts.

We have skewed our nature so much that we don't even know what it feels like to be natural. The concept of sin is artificial; it is the creation of certain doctrines to control our natures based on the incorrect assumption that we are beasts. We are not. It is the doctrines that ingrain guilt and inferiority complexes that will transform us into beasts. Our unique natural constitutions are diverse, which creates the beauty of life. Nothing can stop nature, the Tao, or Brahman, if you will, not even Confucius, Jesus, or Muhammad. Our li is the natural expression of the Tao.

To try and interfere with the Tao is an ill-fated endeavor. But alas, we have been attempting this for thousands of years, and the consequences have been dire. We fervently establish our own sense of morality and impose it on others. But if differing parts of the world have differing moral norms and values, who is to say who has the superior viewpoint?

WHOSE MORALITY IS RIGHT?

Personally, I believe in Swami Vivekananda's vision of an interfaith harmony of all religions, as he is famously known for introducing in his Chicago address to the Parliament of the World's Religions in 1893. But this vision is only possible if two persistent illusions are dissolved: the doctrinal or scriptural privilege of the Abrahamic religions and the end of radical universalism.

The End of Doctrinal Privilege

First point, the interfaith harmony of all religions depends on Christianity and Islam, in particular, eradicating their doctrinal privilege—the belief that the world is split between sinners and the saved based on religion. To have true harmony we must have mutual respect and accept all religions for their own traditions based on their cultural evolution without undermining other religions. This means religious conversion must be abolished, because who is one tradition to superimpose their morality and beliefs on another? To genuinely live in harmony, we must accept each other and employ en masse the path of noninterference, wu-wei, especially considering that is the way of nature and not isolated to a religion. For this to occur, we need mutual respect and acceptance, but more than just tolerating other religions.

In regard to interreligious tension around the world, we often hear the need for religious tolerance thrown around by representatives of many religions. Rajiv Malhotra, a researcher, scientist, and public intellectual on current affairs, world religions, and cross-cultural encounters, valiantly tried to change the dialogue from religious tolerance to mutual respect. In the late 1990s, Malhotra was invited to the inauguration of a major interfaith initiative at Claremont Graduate University. At the event, each representative endorsed a resolution to understand each faith better and declared religious tolerance as a means to achieve this end. But when it was Malhotra's time to speak, he threw the idea of tolerance on its head so that we could make way for mutual respect:

> When it was my turn to speak, I recommended that the term "tolerance" in the resolution be replaced with the phrase "mutual respect." This elicited applause similar to that which had followed the remarks of the other speakers. Then I went on to explain the significance of this change and why this was not a matter of mere semantics.
>
> As I noted, we "tolerate" those we consider not good enough, but we do not extend our respect to them. "Tolerance" implies

control over those who do not conform to our norms by allowing them some, though not all, of the rights and privileges we enjoy. A religion which involves the worship of "false gods" and whose adherents are referred to as "heathens" can be tolerated, but it cannot be respected. Tolerance is a patronizing posture, whereas respect implies that we consider the other to be equally legitimate—a position which some religions routinely deny to others, instead declaring these "others" to be "idol worshippers" or "infidels" and the like.

I wondered aloud if anyone in the audience would like to be told at the upcoming luncheon that he or she was being "tolerated" at the table. No husband or wife would appreciate being told that his or her presence at home was being "tolerated." No self-respecting worker accepts mere tolerance from colleagues. Tolerance, in short, is an outright insult; it is simply not good enough. I pointed out that this notion of tolerance had emerged from religions built on exclusivist claims according to which other religions are false. Hence, tolerating them is the best one can do without undermining one's own claim to exclusivity.

Religious "tolerance" was advocated in Europe after centuries of religious wars between adherents of the different denominations of Christianity. In many European countries, Churches functioned as religious monopolies according to which the mere practice of the "wrong" religion was a criminal offence. "Tolerance" was a positive attempt to quell violence that had plagued Christianity for centuries in Europe, but it did not provide a genuine basis for real unity and cooperation, and so it often broke down.[4]

Similarly, the great Swami Dayananda Saraswati supported the change of language in the resolution from "tolerance" to "mutual respect" at the United Nation's Millennium Religion Summit in 2000. He knew the time had come for non-Judeo-Christian religions to be officially respected as equals and not just tolerated by the Abrahamic religions. As a result, there were serious disagreements over the final language of the resolution to be passed that would usher in the harmony of all religions in the new millennium. Swami Dayananda Saraswati was steadfast despite a lot of pressure. At the last minute, Cardinal Joseph Ratzinger, the then representative of the Vatican (who was also known as Pope Benedict), flinched, and the resolution was passed that all religions would agree to respect each other. However within a month of the summit concluding, the Vatican's Congregation for the Doctrine of the Faith (an office previously known as the Inquisition) issued a new policy on religious pluralism, which reaffirmed the Catholic Church's mission of exclusivity. This was obviously a backward step in the ongoing battle to establish the interfaith harmony of all religions.

Sadly, Malhotra's attempt to establish the essential ingredient of mutual respect for interfaith harmony has been constantly shut down by exclusivist religions. Discarding the doctrinal privilege of the Abrahamic religions is the true way forward for the interfaith harmony of all religions. But, as Malhotra states, the idea of mutual respect may be a bridge too far for those religions that believe their fellow brothers and sisters are mere heathens:

> I have found that people who represent Judeo-Christian faiths are also generally reluctant to reject the mutual respect principle publicly, and yet once the details of the non-Judeo-Christian religions are explained unapologetically, they feel uncomfortable, for deep down they know that their religion demands not only the rejection of such heretical practices and beliefs but their outright destruction.[5]

He poignantly concludes:

After all, if religions deemed "heathen" were to start getting officially respected, there would be no justification for evangelizing and converting their adherents to Christianity. This would undermine the exclusive claims of Christianity which form the justification for the Church's large-scale proselytizing campaigns.[6]

The End of Radical Universalism and Political Thinking

The second point is that the idea of radical universalism must be reevaluated. Scholars, such as Aldous Huxley, did a great job in explaining the perennial philosophy of all spiritual traditions, but that view should not be then extrapolated to assume that all religions are the same or share the same philosophical frameworks and beliefs. They surely don't. Hindu scholar, and a key figure in the Hindu renaissance in India, Ram Swarup was instrumental in exposing the falsity of Mahatma Gandhi's and Jawaharlal Nehru's beliefs that all religions are the same. They are not, though this doesn't negate the good both achieved in the independence of India; it just means this belief is incorrect and misleading.

Ram Swarup brought to the attention of public discourse that Islam and Christianity are actually opposed to Hinduism, and they are truly political philosophies rather than spiritual. Swarup was ostracized for his beliefs during his life, though now, when the damage both religions have had on the Hindu psyche is known to be immense, his opinions are more openly valued. In saying that, India is a place where there are many religions, and they all coexist due to the plurality and acceptance of the Hindu consciousness. As Rajiv Malhotra states:

Indian traditions embody the approach of difference with mutual respect based on the radical idea that differences are not a problem to be solved. Differences are merely characteristics of the way things naturally are, and comfort with them is built into dharmic world views—views which encompass "chaos," doubt, and numerous other complexities.[7]

Forcing one moral perspective over another can only cause conflict. Our whole world has fallen into this trap to differing degrees during history. When we do the bidding of the ideology, we tear at the fabric of our intrinsic connection to each other. We essentially are fighting for our own version of morality under the pretense that we are trying to bring justice. But again, justice according to whose morality? What makes our perspective *the* perspective? We are so afraid to examine these questions because they expose the falsity and hypocrisy of morality itself. The answers are self-explanatory to a Taoist, but a moralist will make up all sorts of excuses or point to some perceived injustice according to their version of morality to justify their cause.

In the modern world, the immorality of morality manifests in numerous forms due to the complexity and confusion of the present day. For example, social justice warriors (SJWs), as they have been labeled, are anxiously trying to end injustice, perceived through a modern illogical lens of ideology. This movement may have begun with good intentions decades prior, but it has devolved into anger and violence based on its own version of injustice. That very movement is popularly known as wokeism and it is frequently used as a tool for hate mongers who try to divide humanity using religion, race, gender, sexuality, and more to suit their own beliefs. As a result, wokeism, just like Confucianism, creates the very problems it seeks to resolve. It is a perfect example of how morality produces its opposite.

Essentially, woke ideology and other ideologies of its ilk are based on post-modernist ideals that are related to Marxism. These post-modernist ideals erode democracy, as everything is reduced to social justice and the division of people into groups rather than one's civic duty to a world they are connected to. This parasitic ideology is the same Marxist or communist doctrine that led to millions of slaughtered people in China and Tibet during the Cultural Revolution due to Mao Zedong's intolerance toward religious freedom. As a result, both Taoism and Buddhism bear the scars of a dangerous belief system gaining momentum and in the wrong hands. That future has the potential to occur in the West with such a modern, divisive ideology. Ironically, those who try and propagate divisive ideologies will likely hate the world they end up living in because the very freedom they had to express their divisive hate will be taken away, as we witness in modern China. The freedom of speech some ideologies are so eager to censor will be the same freedom that they will lose in the spread of their divisiveness.

Marxism doesn't work and the world bears the scars of its violent past. Nothing could be more anti-Taoist, anti-natural. Taking people's freedoms away to suit a tiny minority who have been duped by the media, tech companies, and investment firms based on what this ideology deems as just will not end well. Not allowing people to think and believe what they want, based on one group's version of reality, can lead to fascism. The obvious question no one asks is, why does Silicon Valley get to decide what the world should think? Why don't we follow the beliefs of Bangladesh? Burkina Faso? Guyana? Bhutan? Seriously, why not any of these countries? Who gets to decide? The reality is that the out-of-touch people with power don't reflect the worldview of over 99.99 percent of the world's population. But here we are, where their ideology and technology push people to warp their nature. And yes, it seems the height of insecurity to not allow people and other cultures to have their own worldviews. Only a tyrant believes otherwise. There is no hiding from this fact; you either believe in natural freedom or you believe in a society controlled and censored. There is no middle ground.

Taoism is mature enough to realize that you can't go around and right every wrong and that our past is not something anyone should feel guilty for but rather that everything is a lesson learned, so we can eventually live peacefully in the present moment. As author, economist, and social commentator Thomas Sowell mentioned in a well-known statement in regard to the illusion of coming to a perfect outcome, "There are no solutions, there are only trade-offs; and you try to get the best trade-off you can get, that's all you can hope for."

A fundamental problem with any movement is it is fighting *for* something and so it has a side and justifies its stance based on injustice, which is ironic because the same injustice they are fighting for was created by that very same mindset in the first place. Two wrongs never make a right. If someone is fighting for a cause, then they are creating division based on their own subjective agenda. This subjective agenda unfortunately tends to be related to political ideologies and religions. So woke ideology and the Abrahamic religions are the same in the sense that they are intolerant of other beliefs, and, as a result, lack mutual respect for all people and cultures, just as Rajiv Malhotra explained.

If we all weren't fighting for something then we'd all just be getting along, which is the path of true progress. Real progress is not some illogical ideology based on the illusion of separation.

The main problem with SJWs and wokeism is they breed more division. They still have an agenda, and most agendas breed conflict and are inherently violent. Not to mention they are manipulated by and essentially the creation of big tech companies, the media, and the investment firms that fund them, who all have a vested interest in dividing humanity. As internal arts teacher Damo Mitchell states:

It is possible to form your view of the world and society from your direct experience rather than the view that is given to you by the media and government. Before you open your mouth and express a divisive view, ask yourself if it comes from your direct experience or from some media source that has a vested interest in keeping people divided.[8]

Another modern example is the Western obsession with dualistic, left versus right political views. Both arms of politics have become fundamentalist in their membership. Both fervently oppose the other and will do anything to be the overarching power. From a Taoist perspective, the idea of left versus right is bunk, as it is based on the illusion that there are "categorized" liberal and conservative people. This is the brainchild of the Western cognitive style of individualism, which focuses on categories and objects. From the holistic cognitive style of Taoism, the notion of universal opposites is childish. There is no universal way of thinking either liberally or conservatively. We actually flip-flop through both ways of thinking all the time. To assume we are individually 100 percent liberal or conservative seems ridiculous. Westerners, especially, would benefit from refraining from the habit of categorization and compartmentalization so that we can realize that reality and our minds are much more fluid than we think.

The politicization of the world makes you forget how naturally fluid your mind is, and instead hardwires you into a way of thinking in opposites, which does nothing for unity but rather trains one to be radicalized in a conditioned worldview. Taoism is the red pill for such political absurdity, breaking the illusion. Taoism subverts all types of moral sensibilities, making it the most politically incorrect philosophy in the world. Thank God! What a breath of fresh air. A step away from political divisiveness is always a step in the right direction.

Essentially, most belief systems are built on duality. That is how politics spreads. But the Tao is naturally nondual. Taoism is apolitical because it is amoral and so it has no agenda to spread, nor does it have an ideology that it is bound by. Taoism is the ideology of no ideology, but even this understanding would be to put it in a box and diminish its impartial nature.

Taoism is that natural methodology that is in sync with nature's fluidity, having the variation to move in harmony with life. That is why Taoism raises its eyebrows when witness to all moral opposition in the world. When we fight for a certain cause, we often create monsters who oppose our views, and those people we believe are monsters are nothing but a reflection of who we have become in staunchly adhering to our own beliefs. This should be a no-brainer, but is hard for a stern moralist to realize.

The moralist's weapon is guilt by association, no matter what association. They want you to identify with it when, in reality, it has nothing to do with you. A true Taoist won't fall for such lame attempts to make them obedient. The Taoist lives in the real world, where one is endowed by nature, not human beings or their moral codes. The natural Taoist attitude is not to fight for anything, but instead, to let life be and leave the world alone.

THE AMORAL REALITY

When I think of the amoral attitude of leaving the world alone, I often think of South and Southeast Asia. I have spent many years in both parts of the world, and they have had a positive impact on my life. I am not alone here. When people from all around the world visit such countries as India, Thailand, and Nepal, there is a great sense of relief due to the relaxation of rules and regulations in those nations. You feel all of the tension loosen up in your nervous system.

For some people, it is the first time they've experienced that type of ease in their life. They are no longer wound up. I've known people who think they are pretty chill, but then they spend a few months in Chiang Mai, Thailand, where they, too, realize they were living their whole life with a subtle form of tension from long-term exposure to stress and anxiety in their home country. The rules and regulations based on a certain culture's version of morality tend to box us in, imprisoning our minds. Essentially, governments don't trust people and are run on the illusion that we are beasts from birth, so we need to be told what to do and how to be. Seemingly they have never considered that rules and regulations themselves created and continue to create beasts.

In South and Southeast Asia, on the other hand, rules and regulations are relaxed to allow common sense to take precedence in our way of thinking. This doesn't mean that regulations don't exist at all; rather it just means that everything is not black and white, which reflects the Hindu and Buddhist heritage of that part of the world.

Collective harmony based on common sense is considered first over rules and regulations. Part of their common sense is a trust in people due to the belief in karma. Now, obviously some people take liberty with karma or reject it altogether, but the general consciousness is firmly entrenched in the law of karma. In Thailand, for example, it is very rare that someone would steal another's property. The honor system is highly valued, and I've experienced that first hand from living there for many years. The Thai people don't need to be told not to steal; they need no religious commandments to reinforce their natural inclination toward honoring other people through the natural law of karma.

However, back in the Warring States period, Lao-tzu had to contest with the stiff rules and regulations of Confucianism. Confucius was hellbent on creating rules so that we would have charity and duty toward others because, after all, we are beasts. In an imaginary dialogue created by Chuang-tzu, Lao-tzu challenges Confucius's attempt at creating a system of morality to make people *natural* and *pious*:

> "Tell me," said Lao-tzu, "in what consists charity and duty to one's neighbour?"
>
> "They consist," answered Confucius, "in a capacity for rejoicing in all things; in universal love, without the element of self. These are the characteristics of charity and duty to one's neighbour."
>
> "What stuff!" cried Lao-tzu. "Does not universal love contradict itself? Is not your elimination of self a positive manifestation of self? Sir, if you would cause the empire not to lose its source of nourishment, there is the universe, its regularity is unceasing; there are the sun and moon, their brightness is unceasing; there are the stars, their groupings never change; there are the birds and beasts, they flock together without varying; there are the trees and shrubs, they grow upward without exception. Be like these: follow Tao, and you will be perfect. Why then these vain struggles after charity and duty to one's neighbour, as though beating a drum in search of a fugitive. Alas! Sir, you have brought much confusion into the mind of man."[9]

Lao-tzu illustrates the dangers of Confucius's imposed morality on the masses, because we slowly but surely lose our true nature and become out of sync with nature (if only he could see the world today). Lao-tzu's point is if Confucius never created a moral system to follow, then there would be no need for charity and duty. All would be well and essentially similar to my example of the ease of restrictions in South and Southeast Asia.

We are not beasts, so our charity and duty to others is not based on some mandate, but rather a natural inclination we have toward collective harmony.

Rules and guidelines based on morality breed an artificial separation among people. A pious standard creates division and hierarchy. Those who can play the game of morality well in life succeed, and the rest just have to try and work it out for themselves. Moral standards bring judgment and that leads to a world divided. Basically, more morals, more fear. We are constantly living in fear because we are trying to live up to inhumane standards daily. Hence Westerners, especially, feel a sense of ease when escaping a heightened version of morality in their home countries.

A Taoist sage is a pure reflection of nature, and so they need no rules. They are naturally charitable, generous, and kind. The Taoist sage also doesn't add fuel to the fire with an interventionist approach. As a pure reflection of nature, they are not touched by the drama of the world. They are not consumed by the fear morality creates and so, as a result, it is far easier for them to allow life to be because they are no longer a victim of the socialization process. They have escaped the social spin that we are beasts from birth. The real amoral world the Taoist sage lives in is where we allow nature to be without conditioning it or molding it to a socialization process. We must stick to the uncarved block and leave life alone.

This means we stop interfering with the way of nature because any form of interference is laced with our own personal agenda based on the culture and morality we believe we are part of. We cannot escape this agenda if we subscribe to a conditioned belief system. It is part and parcel of morality itself. Our best intentions are often the worst for another. When we try to manufacture goodness, we create oppression, not to mention we are not authentic in our intentions. Our goodness is not true goodness from the heart, but rather a goodness based on an external morality.

From the amoral view of Taoism, goodness is not something we can cultivate but rather is an inherent quality to human beings. This is best articulated by Mencius's child-and-well metaphor (孟軻: Wade-Giles *Meng-tzu*; Pinyin *Mengzi*; 372–289 BCE). Even though Mencius is considered a Confucian, he was much more Taoist than we think. His perspective of innate goodness is in alignment with Lao-tzu and Taoism. In the story, Mencius uses a child fetching water from a well to evoke this innate goodness within all of us. Picture yourself in this story as a bystander. You watch a child go to the well to retrieve water. The weight of the bucket is too heavy, and the child is about to fall into the well. What would be your instinctual reaction? Most of us would do anything humanly possible to stop the child from falling in the well. That instinctual response is our spontaneous nature beneath our rationality. The situation requires a spontaneous response, and ours, as Mencius points out, is naturally good. We'll do anything to save the child. We are just hardwired that way.

What the child-and-well story illustrates is that our innate goodness connects us to the world in a harmonious way. We are naturally calibrated to the world, but we unfortunately sever this harmony when we create artificial systems of morality that bore holes into our faces. Mencius again has another metaphor to explain beautifully how our innate goodness is eclipsed by socialization, creating toxic people. This is the famous Ox Mountain story. In the story, Mencius and a student were debating whether human nature is fundamentally good. The student was talking about all the mountains in the area, all of which are lush and green except for Ox Mountain, which is barren and desolate. The student's point was that because Ox Mountain is desolate, its nature is fundamentally bad. Mencius's counterargument reveals a glaring fact that the student overlooked. Mencius points out the close proximity of Ox Mountain to a large country:

> The woods on Ox Mountain were once beautiful! On account of its being on the edge of a large country, it had been attacked with axes and hatchets, and then how could it remain beautiful? The refreshing breezes of day and night, and the moisture provided by rain and fog, did not fail to give rise to sprouts of vegetation. But cows and sheep have been repeatedly pastured there, and for that reason it has remained desolate. People observe its denuded state and assume that it never had any good resources. But how could this state be the true nature of this mountain?[10]

Ox Mountain's nature was not fundamentally bad; it was the environment that surrounded it that was toxic. All of those years on the edge of a large country made it appear toxic externally, but internally the sprouts continued to grow. Mencius's point is that Ox Mountain is a metaphor for how human beings truly are within. So "bad" people are not innately bad; they are just a product of toxic environments that shift their innate goodness in a different direction, essentially distorting their nature. But that doesn't mean we shouldn't be accountable for our own actions; of course we should. However, the fact is we were all innately good from birth.

We are all like Ox Mountain one way or the other. If you're reading these words, then you've surely gone through a socialization process. Once we accept the ideologies forged upon us, we become barren and desolate just like Ox Mountain. But no matter how warped your nature is, your fundamental goodness is still within, maybe suppressed so deep within you that it's not visible, but it's still there.

If only we could leave Ox Mountain alone. Imagine if we did; its nature would come back to life and nourish all other life around it. We, too, will come back to life if we leave others alone to grow and thrive as nature intended. Instead of interfering with someone's nature, leave them be. This not only has a positive effect on others but also yourself as you begin to embrace the Taoist principle of amorality. And once we come back to our amoral nature, we realize that socialization nurtures a fundamental cognitive error that distorts our view of the reality we experience.

5

Beyond Good and Evil

Nature is impartial to all things, and we are nature. But as we go through the socialization process, our perception of life is trained in partiality. Our mind essentially doesn't experience life as nature intended for us. As a result, we require a system of morality to govern our distorted view of the world. It is a continuous cycle beginning with socialization, then our distorted partial view of the world, and last with a system of morality to govern what that indoctrination created, and on and on we go in an infinite hypnotic cycle.

Astonishingly, we sit around all day and wonder why our world is the way it is, but most never consider if our view of reality is distorted. As Confucius twisted our nature to somehow try and be natural, so does any form of socialization distort our nature to see the world in its image. This infuses a fundamental cognitive error, where the impartial reality of nature is dissected at the hands of the partiality of socialization. This is the birth of "this" and "that," the superimposition of a linguistic framework to categorize forms with names. In Buddhism this is known as the Sanskrit term *namarupa* (nama means "name" or "mental component" and rupa means "form" or "physical component"). But it is within Taoism that we discover why this cognitive error occurs.

THE BIRTH OF THIS AND THAT

In Chinese there is a word called *qing* (情: Wade-Giles *ch'ing*; Pinyin *qing*). Qing can mean a variety of things, such as emotions, feelings, or sentiment. But Chuang-tzu explained qing in a different way; he said qing is a species-specific essence, which is based on the Mohist logical theory of Mo-tzu* (墨子: Wade-Giles *Mo-tzu*; Pinyin *Mozi*; 470–391 BCE). Qing is a defining characteristic of a species. For example, the grace of a horse's gallop is its qing, or the enormous hop of a kangaroo is its qing. We could use numerous examples to highlight this species-specific essence. But what about us? What about human beings? Chuang-tzu makes a startling revelation about our qing that explains the confusion we often live in; it is a flaw.

Chuang-tzu stated thousands of years ago that our species-specific essence is a flaw. So what is our qing? Our qing, according to Chuang-tzu, is our ability to discern between "this" and "that." Qing is our ability to intellectually dissect the world up into pieces, and this qing is nurtured by socialization that, in actuality, was created due to this human flaw or cognitive error.

The way we perceive the world is through the partial lens of qing. The reason why Chuang-tzu explained qing as a human flaw is because all sorts of invalid views of the world arise from a mind riddled with the cognitive error of interpreting the world through the discernment of this and that. All of our likes and dislikes arise from our qing. Our view of good and evil is the result of our qing, and, paradoxically, we apply a system of morality to govern our human

---

*Mohist logical theory is part of Mohism. Mohism was an ancient Chinese philosophy during the Warring States period based on logic, rational thought, and science developed by academic scholars who studied under the ancient Chinese philosopher Mo-tzu.

flaws, and it's all built on the illusion that the world is separate and partial as defined by our own version of this and that.

Socialization, then, nurtures our flaw of discerning the world into this and that with no nuance, adding what is right and wrong according to the overarching society, culture, and religion. Our human flaw of qing is colored by social indoctrination, and we then live in an illusory world that we feel is real. It is not. The world frankly is not what we think because the way we think has been hacked. Socialization manipulates our human flaws for its own ends. The overarching social system rarely has your best interests at heart, as we see with the cultivation of competing forms of morality and divisive ideologies. And these competing forms of morality are built on our own version of right and wrong, which are both a byproduct of our qing.

Our conditioning influences our qing, and our conditioning is colored by socialization. What we see is not reality itself, but a world according to our conditioning. We superimpose our beliefs of separation onto a world that is sincerely whole and one. This builds an illusion of the world in our mind, and we act and react according to the way we see the world, which is not the true view of the world. What we see, according to the human flaw of qing, is a projection of our own version of the world—a world we've created from the external cues from society and our own culture. We essentially imbue a unified reality with the color of duality based on our binary mind. This builds an illusory reality in our mind that most experience their entire lives without ever waking up from the dream. This is the illusion of *maya* revealed by the ancient rishis of India.

THE ILLUSORY MENTAL PROJECTION

Maya in Sanskrit literally means "illusion." The Sanskrit root of maya is *ma* and *matr*, which both mean "measurement" and are also the root of the Greco-Latin words matrix, meter, and matter. So maya essentially means "the illusion of reality we create by measuring reality." Maya is identical to qing in the sense that the illusion of reality is created by the measurement of this and that, which creates an infinitude of separation and, as a result, suffering (the majority of humanity live in maya and don't even know it). Maya, then, more succinctly is a construct, a subjective reality we build in our minds. Actually, construction is a more accurate description of maya than illusion, as mythologist Devdutt Pattanaik explains:

> Construction means a perception of the world shaped by a measuring scale that depends on cultural norms and personal prejudices. This perception changes every time there is a change in cultural norms or personal prejudices. What is considered right or good or beautiful today may not be considered so tomorrow, all sensory inputs remain the same. Thus the perception can be "de-constructed" and "re-constructed." The word *illusion* came from typical scientific arrogance that logic can decipher the truth free of all bias. The word *construction* admits that all understanding is rooted in bias.
>
> For Hindus, maya is a constructed reality.[1]

Maya is a constructed reality in our mind based on the measuring scale of qing that values and devalues all things in nature. As a result, this gives rise to an individual's own subjective view of the world, which is out of sync with the way nature truly is. The subjective world constructed by maya is known in Sanskrit as *Brahmanda*, according to Pattanaik. Everyone has their own Brahmanda, their own "subjective view of the world." Brahmanda itself is the socialization process that seeks to mold nature; in this context, *Prakriti* is the Sanskrit word for nature. As Pattanaik explains:

Prakriti is nature. Brahmanda is culture. Prakriti creates man. Man creates Brahmanda. Prakriti is objective reality. Brahmanda is subjective reality. Atma witnesses Prakriti, aham constructs Brahmanda.[2]

Atman (Atma) is the "undifferentiated consciousness that perceives nature as it is," while *aham* is "the ego that creates its own world due to qing and socialization." This ego, as mentioned in chapter three, is the accumulative sense of self, the isolated identity. And this subjective reality is Brahmanda in Hinduism. Brahmanda is split into three worlds: me, mine, and what is not mine. These three worlds can also be referred to as the natural world, the cultural world, and the personal world. The three worlds also mean the three bodies according to the *Sharira Traya*, the *Doctrine of the Three Bodies* in Hinduism: *sthula sharira* (gross body), *sukshma sharira* (subtle body, including the conscious mind full of opinions), and *karana sharira* (causal body, including the unconscious mind full of impressions that affect our habits and tendencies, which are the *samskaras* and *vasanas*).

All in all, these three worlds are known in Sanskrit as *Tripura*, which are symbolized by the blades of Shiva's trident. The Tripura are the three constructed realities we occupy because of maya. Each of these three worlds are mortal and eclipse our vision of the nondual Tao. The "me," as part of the natural world, is made up of the body and mind. The "mine" is made up of the knowledge, relationships, wealth, status, and property we claim ownership over and assume we control. The "not mine" is made up of everything else in the world that we don't have ownership over and are unable to control.

We continually identify with these three worlds, and so we are under the spell of maya. Our perception of reality is shaped by these three worlds. But as with anything that is constructed,

Shiva Lingam with Tripundra

it can also be deconstructed. The secrets of this deconstruction are symbolized by Shiva's trident and Shiva himself. Although the three blades of the trident represent the three worlds of Tripura, it is the staff of the trident that holds the key to our liberation. The staff of Shiva's trident symbolizes the staff of wisdom. The staff is the *lingam* beyond maya. The Shiva lingam is a famous symbol in Shaivism, which represents the actual nondual reality of Brahman, the ultimate reality.

Shiva uses the trident, the staff of wisdom, to destroy the three worlds of Brahmanda that the measuring scale of maya constructed. When we destroy the me, mine, and not mine with wisdom, we arise from the ashes and mark ourselves with Shiva's sacred mark, the *Tripundra* in Sanskrit—the three horizontal lines of ash a Shaiva smears on their forehead (a Shaiva is a devotee of Shiva). Ash is an important symbol in Shaivism, as it represents that which survives when matter is destroyed. Ash essentially symbolizes the Atman that was never born and can never die. The three lines, then, symbolize the three worlds that are deconstructed, or destroyed, by Shiva's third eye of wisdom. The third eye is the perception that is not colored by the flaw of qing, the construction of maya.

Shiva symbolizes the deconstruction of maya. Shiva is often thought of as a destroyer, but a more accurate description is that Shiva deconstructs the illusory mental world we have projected onto a natural world devoid of categorization. We deconstruct our subjective world by being conscious of how we measure reality according to our conditioning, which arose from our qing. It is this constant measurement of reality that causes all conflict and confusion within us and the world.

All sorts of artificial divisions and illusions of separation are the result of this measurement. Our likes and dislikes, beliefs, culture, and ideologies are all based on qing. When this is explained to a politically oriented righteous person, they can become sensitive and aggressive because this view of reality suggests that theirs is essentially fake. This is why moralists in general can be very aggressive and undermining toward Eastern spirituality, because it goes against their entire world view. Thankfully, though, Taoism, Buddhism, and Hinduism have survived for thousands of years to provide clarity and sanity in an increasingly unstable world. Throughout the ages, Eastern spirituality explored the science of consciousness to provide a solution to the measurement problem.

THE ETERNAL WORLD
BEYOND MEASUREMENT

The measuring scale of this and that eclipses the true nature of the world and consciousness itself. The Tao is that eternal reality beyond the dualistic measurement of the mind. The Tao is imma-nent within the world but also transcends it. The construction of maya that the flaw of qing creates must be torn down to align with the Tao. Once we deconstruct our subjective reality and cease the habit of this and that, then we will abide in a reality where the infi-nite in all life is felt and sensed. As Chuang-tzu explains:

> *When there is no more separation between "this" and "that," it is called the still-point of the Tao. At the still-point in the center of the circle one can see the infinite in all things.*[3]

To achieve such a heightened state of consciousness, one must apply a strong level of discernment over the contents of one's mind to renounce the contents of the mind. Our awareness must return to its pure stillness (wu chi) to see the world impartially so that we let go of the partiality that was essentially learned. In Advaita Vedanta, there is a philosophy and practice that correlates to Chuang-tzu's teaching of qing and the infinite in all things. This philosophy and practice are known in Sanskrit as *neti neti*, meaning "not this, not this," or "not this, not that."

There are two interpretations of neti neti that can be seen as different or part of the whole philosophy and practice. The first understanding is the more common one that people encounter, which is neti neti, "I am not this body." And this wisdom is true because the body is an impermanent vehicle for the eternal con-sciousness (Atman). Basically, the body is a covering, a meat suit that we incorrectly identify with as if it is our true everlasting nature. A sadhu and yogi take this a step further and renounce the body in a divine act of absorbing their awareness in the Atman, and so, as a result, distance themselves from the body. This is not an easy practice to master and not for beginners, because if you haven't had sufficient training, then this form of neti neti can cause dissociation and psychological problems. To genuinely follow that practice, you have to throw yourself in the fire, so to speak, and give yourself fully to the austere sadhu or yogi path. But this is only one interpretation of neti neti and is actually not the deeper essence of the teaching going back to the ancient Vedas (also, it could be noted from a differing perspective that making a distinction between the body and the Atman is duality itself and not the nonduality of the whole).

The core teaching in Advaita Vedanta is not physical renunciation, but rather mental renunciation. This is the elimination of the flaw of qing, the innate habit of discerning between this and that, hence "not this, not that." To enhance mental renunciation, one must also practice *viveka* ("discrimination and discernment between the real and unreal in our mind" in Sanskrit) and *vairagya* ("renunciation, nonreaction, or dispassion" in Sanskrit). Viveka is applied to discriminate and discern between the real and the illusion, which means the ability to abide as the undifferentiated Atman and witness the temporary ego or identity. Harnessing viveka is made possible by vairagya because when we renounce and not react to the power of distractions around us in the world, we can abide in our pure stillness of mind, and so we can see reality as it honestly is.

Vairagya and viveka allow us to see clearly how we fragment reality through this and that. As a result, as we apply neti neti, we begin to withdraw from the illusion of right and wrong and good and bad that we have developed in our mind from incorrect seeing. One person's version of good is another's version of evil. They are not intrinsic; they are dependent on perspective. And anything in the field of this or that is not natural, not how the world truly is, not reflective of a state of wholeness or oneness.

THE FOUR PILLARS OF SEPARATION

Our belief in good and evil or right and wrong is built on the flaw of qing. These beliefs in separation are molded by the socialization process according to differing systems of morality. We then incorrectly identify with the distorted view resulting from qing and socialization. All conflict and confusion arise from here. When we believe in these incorrect associations, violence is inevitable. The common four pillars of separation of religion, nation, race, and sex are what tend to cause the most conflict and confusion in the world. We overly associate and become a fundamentalist about any of these four pillars, blurring our view of reality. Reality is one, but when we fall for a fundamentalist belief in any of these pillars, then we can do anything in the name of protecting our belief, regardless of the consequences and the harm we inflict on others.

For example, someone may feel their skin color is superior and treat others poorly with the stupid notion that other races are beneath their own. Likewise, someone may feel their skin color is inferior or they have been hard done by, so they play the victim to gain an upper hand and consequently create the same form of racism they opposed. And this is no surprise considering that any belief that you are separate and different from another group is inherently a form of separation. This type of understanding makes those, particularly in the West, who feel they are superior or play the victim according to injustice uncomfortable. This is no surprise when, as discussed earlier, the West is subtly influenced by the moral system of Christianity, which is inherently biased in its view of morality as it is based on the inhumane righteousness of Christ. As a result, Westerners have to give their *two cents* all the time, as if their opinions matter more than others'. Westerners are very firm in their views, and they don't mind telling you about them. And Westerners of any race have the same moralistic tendency, the "we know best" attitude. That Western analytical cognition has nothing to do with skin color, but rather culture.

Cultural programming is the reason why the idea of global racial communities is an illusion (not to mention race itself is an illusion). Black people in Louisiana in the United States are vastly different from the Masai people of Tanzania. Likewise, white people in North Queensland in Australia are vastly different from white people in Siberia, Russia. On top of this, you have the Far East Asian people of Korea, China, and Japan, with very different cultures that don't identify with each other. The only similarity of all three examples is the amount of melanin one has, and we incorrectly identify with that skin color. But our skin color is not a football jersey and a team we are part of, even though, sadly, many people view it that way. Also, there is no one black or white race, for example. There are numerous races and so the idea of black and white people is incorrect and doesn't make sense really. Africa and Europe alone have many different races that we inappropriately lump into broad categories (a terrible Western cognitive habit). It wasn't so long ago that a genocide against the Jews in Europe occurred, and many people in this day and age ignorantly lump the Jews into the broad category of the "white race." Adolf Hitler saw this differently and suffered from the illusion of racial communities, and, sadly, we live to tell the tragic events of World War II. We can avoid any future calamities if we wake up and understand race is an illusion.

As human beings, we are much deeper and more extraordinary than the differing amounts of melanin we have in our outer shell. And even though some people from all around the world may have similar skin colors, that doesn't mean they belong to that group, because it isn't a cohesive, singular group in the first place. Actually, there have been many social psychology experiments in the United States that vary skin color and accents, and it is accent that holds the most power (as it is an important part of culture), not skin color. As social psychologist Jonathan Haidt explains:

> People aren't going to dislike you just because you have different skin color. Prejudice tends to be more about judgments of behavior and values than simple physical differences. It's [accents holding power over race] what you would guess about what that person is going to be like, again, with an eye towards cooperation and trust. We're always trying to size up, is this someone I want to trust and work with.[4]

As a seasoned traveler, I've seen this firsthand where people will make a connection based on accent, not race. Often travelers have many different skin colors, but they identify with the accent and don't consider appearance (considering friendship based on appearance is really shallow and strange anyway). Living in India, I witnessed this firsthand when Indian-born Indians and American-born Indians would have little in common, especially if the American-born Indian was not Hindu. It is more about cultural programming than anything else.

This is also the case with the sexes. Just like race, we can incorrectly build and believe in inequality through the belief that one sex is superior and one inferior based on the systems of morality we are indoctrinated with. The belief that you are this singular sex fundamentally, resulting in a division from one half of the planet, can develop within either sex. There are differences between males and females, both psychologically and physically, due, for example, to elevated levels of the hormone testosterone in men (as well as a host of other things). Your sexual organs affect your psychology. Though, these differences may affect people to a greater or lesser degree, you are biologically a man or woman nonetheless, and we revert easily back to our biology in a survival situation. This is nature. But that doesn't mean there is a fundamental separation between the sexes; rather, it means people, no matter the sex, are equipped in different ways to facilitate life and bring harmony to the world. Actually, as we all know too well, the union of female and male creates life; there is just no other way to enter this world. When the mutually arising opposites are one, we create life. There is a real divine beauty in the natural connection between men and women that is hard to describe, as it is profoundly sacred.

Through an embrace of wholeness and oneness, sentient life, not just humans, creates the magic of the universe. But, as with race, when we overly identify with either sex as if it is our team, then we develop this hypnosis that we belong only to that community, when in fact, for example, a woman from one side of the planet may identify more with the men from her familiar culture than another woman from the other side of the planet who only shares her biology and fundamental psychology. Race and sex are artificial divisions from the nondual consciousness of Tao—overly identified with when one is under the delusion of qing, the magical spell of maya. This is enhanced by the two major pillars of separation that cause a lot of bloodshed and conflict in the world: nations and religions.

We examined the separation caused by religion in depth in chapter four and similarly nation-states have been a main source of separation in attempts to influence other nation-states and parts of the world. And what is really behind religions and nations is the cultural program that groups of people for millennia have used in the spirit of demographic swamping. One's way of life in one nation, including the religion of that land, is incorrectly assumed to be best for other cultures.

As religions preach conversion based on doctrinal privilege, nationalistic invasions are similarly rooted in the overidentification with one's cultural programming. When we firmly believe we *are* our nation or religion, then this can lead to war and unnecessary bloodshed.

Many people around the world feel a sense of pride when they are a patriot or a religious fundamentalist. But nothing could be more threatening to the peace and harmony of the world. Sadly, being either is praised in a lot of nations and religious communities around the world. This is all due to the illusory belief of identifying yourself with the superficial elements of life that are essentially not who you truly are. The fact of the matter is, the more we identify with the four pillars of separation—religion, nation, race, and sex—the more conflict and division will ensue in the world, separating us further from the truth of our inherent oneness in the Tao as the way.

Nature is harmonious because it is not in conflict with other elements; everything plays its part. Likewise, if we love and accept our superficial differences, we will discover that we are more similar than different, which would be a breeding ground for peace and harmony. Radical acceptance has always been hard for human beings to assimilate, but it is the unchartered territory we must traverse if we are to make it as a species.

A mature humanity understands that, on a superficial level, all so-called differentiations are good because nature provides flavor to produce beauty, and this is why variety is the spice of life. But the spices are contained within nature, which is one. So this flavor can only be spoiled if someone overly identifies with a single one and so, as a result, they become isolated from all other flavor differences and hypnotically believe they are separate from all other differences in nature, and actually separate from nature itself. If we accept nature in all of its glory, on the other hand, then we will become one with the process of nature and experience the beauty of life. Acceptance of the way nature intrinsically exists becomes a gateway to allowing your consciousness to flower in wholeness.

IDENTITY IS FUNDAMENTALLY INSECURE AND LIMITED

Our mind is innately whole, intrinsically one, but our belief in our identity and what we identify with is an illusion. We hypnotically believe that relating with a group leads to security, but in actuality, our yearning for safety based on what we identify with causes division and conflict that didn't exist prior. But this yearning for security is the seed of conflict and basically holds us back from seeing the full picture. It is a limited view of the world.

The common belief is that we will find security in the family, tribe, nation, race, or sex. We believe security is in division. If we identify with a certain group, this will ensure our safety and propagate our limited knowledge. Do you see the inherent flaw in this common perspective? The division itself creates insecurity. Our identification with a group creates the problem. All battles are waged based on the illusory belief that division ensures security. We've drawn a line in the sand saying, "this is who I am and what I believe." But the division itself is limited.

Anything that is limited must inevitably create conflict. This cuts to the heart of the individual. For example, if I say, "I am an individual," it is limited. I'm only concerned with myself, which is finite. I am only concerned about the way I see the world according to my beliefs and conditioning, which are intrinsically divisional. The "me," "I," and "my" are divisive entities. Our yearning for security paradoxically creates an identity that is fundamentally insecure. Do you see the irony? All of the injustice and also the reactions to injustice in the world come from the limited individual. One who hasn't thought about this does not consider the world as a whole. One who doesn't consider themselves as the world instead views themselves as part of it, divided from other parts that conflict with their limited view.

We're mainly concerned about our superficial differences, no matter whether they are religious, cultural, racial, sexual, national, etc. We're not focused on the human condition—the root cause of division. A thorough understanding of the human condition dissolves all illusory dividers and boundaries. Our apparent differences are small in comparison to our intrinsic similarities, which are vast. Sadly, most people cling to their superficial differences. Focusing on these is an act of division, a way of isolating ourselves from the rest of the world as if our identity is real. According to philosopher Jiddu Krishnamurti, this act of separation is violence:

> When you call yourself an Indian or a Muslim or a Christian or a European, or anything else, you are being violent. Do you see why it is violent? Because you are separating yourself from the rest of mankind. When you separate yourself by belief, by nationality, by tradition, it breeds violence. So a man who is seeking to understand violence does not belong to any country, to any religion, to any political party or partial system; he is concerned with the total understanding of mankind.[5]

That act of separation is the cause of all conflict. When I say "I," I naturally create conflict with you because the "I" I believe I am is finite, and likewise you are too. Our limitations can only breed conflict because we have separated ourselves from the whole of humanity. To truthfully understand this fact, we have to admit that we are limited as individuals. In Taoism, there is no "I" without the world because the individual doesn't exist. The "I" is a divisive entity that sustains its illusory existence through insecurity, causing conflict as long as it survives. We need to inquire into the nature of the identity we all believe we are. This identity is fundamentally conditioned, and any form of conditioning is limited.

There are questions we need to ask: What is beneath all of this conditioning? What is the real essence of our being? This has nothing to do with spirituality but rather the fundamental basis of our minds, minus the divisional accumulative identity. The Eastern spiritual traditions have primarily focused on the nature of the mind and consciousness itself. For thousands of years the conclusion was that the doer of actions and the thinker of thoughts causes all the trouble in the world. The belief in "I" can only cause conflict. This "I" identity, with all of its beliefs, agendas, biases, and prejudices, is an illusion. It is an accumulative social construct only useful as a public utility.

When we explore the nature of our minds, we discover that its contents are polluted with learned beliefs about a sense of self we are supposed to be, and a body we are supposed to identify with, as if it's permanent and everlasting. What happens when we explore these beliefs? We realize they were all built on our insecurity and imbued within us from other people suffering the same affliction. Real security, then, is not found in identification with division, but rather found in the sense of unity we feel within with no divisional boundaries. This state of unity is our natural state of mind that we have covered over with the illusion of separation.

Religion, nation, race, and sex reinforce division when we believe that is who we are at a fundamental level. Under this mirage, we will create injustice and react to it without realizing that both opposing views are built on the illusory belief that division ensures security, which is the result of qing, the play of maya. Our actions and reactions are based on the fragmentation of reality that the flaw of qing produces. If we were educated from birth on the nature of consciousness, then world conflict and confusion would be radically reduced. Instead of investing in future generations with tools of separation, why not invest in them knowing that separation is a faulty state of mind? This is where the technology of Taoism could be utilized en masse to reorient our minds back to their natures.

If we don't return to our natures, then we'll probably always operate from an "eye for an eye." But as Gandhi is known to have said, "An eye for an eye makes the whole world blind." Our identification with the illusory components of separation fixates our mind on past indiscretions, no matter how far back in history, and we want to bring justice according to our distorted view of the world, which, in the end, only creates the problems we seek to resolve (not to mention a bunch of other problems as well).

Radical acceptance has been hard for the majority of the world to embody. But we could look to India for inspiration in regard to radical acceptance, which actually demonstrates that India is a representation of Taoist naturalness without claiming it. For example, India, as discussed, has been oppressed for centuries, yet the Indian people don't hold a grudge and have got on with living. If we were to employ Western thinking, we would assume that a British person, for example, traveling to India in the modern day would be met with resistance because of the past. But that is not the case. British people are treated like any other foreigner—with open arms—as, according to Hinduism, we are all, deep down, the ultimate reality of Brahman. Indians hold no ill will and are getting on with life like mature adults. This is all due to their spirituality. Radical acceptance and the dissolution of the illusion of separation and identity are part and parcel with the Hindu culture.

India's spirituality is why the people can deal with anything you throw at them. Their spirituality is built on the deconstruction of maya through practices such as neti neti. Instead of feeding the problem of qing, Hinduism, Taoism, and also Buddhism offer solutions to ground ourselves back into our pure natures. The more we reign in our tendency to dissect the world, the more we'll begin to have a deep sense of wholeness and oneness. This cannot eventuate by adding to our consciousness but rather by subtracting the contents of our mind that were shaped by our fragmented view of reality.

One of the core aspects of Chuang-tzu's fasting the mind teaching is the fasting of qing. When we fast the habit of qing, we begin to see the world as it truly is, rather than through our beliefs, likes, and dislikes. Standing on top of a mountain peak, the Taoist sage sees the infinite in life in its true state of oneness.

THE SAGE'S VISION

To see the world as it genuinely is, we must become an identical representation of nature by returning to our nature. The Taoist sage is the perfected state of nature as it is. They are a mirror of the natural forces of the universe because they have merged as one with the river of Tao, the way of nature. The Taoist sage is as nature is, and this is what is most difficult for most people to embody because what is required is a complete turning away from the partiality of qing. We learn, due to qing and socialization, to cut the world up into pieces to suit our own distorted worldview. Nature, on the other hand, is impartial to all things. Everything is treated equally by nature; it has no bias. As the Tao Te Ching states, "The Tao loves and nourishes all but does not lord it over them."

Nature provides equal plenitude. We all experience the ups and downs of life to differing degrees, and we all surely experience illness and death. We all share these and will experience them. Nature is somewhat like a machine; it is unaware of the effects of its actions. It doesn't care that tornadoes destroy houses, that earthquakes and tsunamis destroy entire communities, nor does nature care that winter destroys what was grown in the summer and spring. The Taoist sage has the same indifferent outlook as nature. They have fasted qing completely from their mind. As a result, they treat everyone equally, no better or worse. In seeing reality as it truly is, the sage has a childlike innocence and suspended judgment. They do not project their beliefs or opinions onto the world because their faculties are empty of qing.

The sage is completely indifferent to the concerns and dramas of the world because they see all equally and have no side to take. They don't add any fuel to an already raging fire. In chapter five of the Tao Te Ching, Lao-tzu accentuates and articulates the dispassionate and nonspecial view of the sage through the Chinese ritual use of straw dogs:

> *Heaven and Earth are impartial*
> *And regard myriad things as straw dogs.*
> *The sages are impartial*
> *And regard people as straw dogs.*[6]

Straw dogs are an important feature of Chinese rituals. They are obviously made of straw and actually don't represent dogs, but rather all living creatures. In the rituals, there is no attachment to straw dogs, they are discarded with utter indifference. This is significant for eliminating our unintelligent anthropocentric view of specialness. We are all part of the straw dogs of Tao, the straw dogs of Heaven and Earth.

Nature discards us with no attachment. You might be special to your family and friends, but no one else really cares. Whoever you are, alive or dead, has no bearing on someone on the other side of the planet. Billions of souls have lived and died on this Earth, but no one can remember their names. This is a sobering truth for our sense of specialness, which should humble even the most egotistical heart. But this is not negative; rather it is positive because when we remove our self-centered view, we begin to open ourselves to the Tao.

The world doesn't love you when you are alive and hate you when you die. Nature is empty of those emotions. Objectively, life and death occur with complete impartiality. No governing God determines your life and death because nature discards its straw dogs without losing any sleep. The deeper lesson in regard to straw dogs is that they are not made for emotions, but instead because they serve a particular function or purpose. The straw dogs of human beings, then, are not here to be confused and lost in their emotions, but rather a human is here to become an aperture for the Tao to express itself. So your particular purpose or function in this life is more about aligning with the fundamental forces of the river of Tao.

Emotions only get in the way of seeing reality as it undeniably exists. Does this mean emotions are inherently bad? No. They can be beautiful, but often they are confused for the reality we are experiencing. Emotions are amplified by qing, which leads to all sorts of conflict. The sage rises above feelings once the mind is fasted back into its original nature. They are dispassionate, based on reasoning rather than emotion. Emotions for the sage still exist, but they are not the motivating factor driving their life.

The Taoist sage rises above preferences and superficiality. They are completely empty and impartial like nature, which corresponds to the emptiness of Sunyata in Buddhism. Even though the sage is empty, their power can never be exhausted. In the Tao Te Ching, the sage's power harnessed by emptiness is likened to the bellows. The bellows, like the sage, is empty but powerful. There seems to be nothing in the bellows, yet its power is inexhaustible. It only contains empty space, but the more you use it, the more blasts of air you produce from it. Likewise, the Tao contains nothing but emptiness, and yet everything emerges from this emptiness. The more the sage opens themselves to Tao, the more powerful and versatile their manifestations become in their life. This can be the same for all of us if we open ourselves to the Tao.

Being an expression of the Tao opens the floodgates of creativity because your mind is empty like the void of Tao, and new ideas emerge from nothingness, as life is born from the void. You'll probably never experience writers block because the Tao is moving through you as you. Your intuitions about the right approach keep coming spontaneously. Your actions are immediate and appropriate in accord with the Tao, giving you the effortless ability to easily navigate through life. Your actions will arise from nothingness, but they have the power of Tao fueling them. You become an intelligent limb of the Tao devoid of emotions that will obscure your vision of the world.

The sage's awareness is analogous to being on top of a mountain peak looking down on the world. From their lofty view, life is a beautiful rhythm, empty of meaning and emotions. They can honestly see that within apparent chaos, there is actually order. The problem is when our awareness is on the ground level, there is only chaos because we have not fasted our mind and began our return up the mountain of Tao. We are caught in qing and constantly suffer as we contribute to the chaos of maya. Billions of worlds (Brahmanda) are constantly clashing; there is no end in sight. But the fact of the matter is what the sage sees is how reality truly is.

Nature is impartial, and any form of partiality, no matter how real it feels, is an illusion. There is only the rhythm of Tao, a divine order witnessed by those sages who have completely fasted their mind of this and that, right and wrong, or good and evil. From our illusion of partiality, we believe the Taoist sage offers nothing to humanity, but as Richard Wilhelm states in his translation and commentary of the I Ching, the sage actually creates incomparable values for the future:

> Not every man has an obligation to mingle in the affairs of the world. There are some who are developed to such a degree that they are justified in letting the world go its own way and in refusing to enter public life with a view to reforming it. But

this does not imply a right to remain idle or to sit back and merely criticize. Such withdrawal is justified only when we strive to realize in ourselves the higher aims of mankind. For although the sage remains distant from the turmoil of daily life, he creates incomparable human values for the future.[7]

Once we empty our mind of qing and the illusion of maya, we begin to live simply as nature is. Our impartial nature is innately simple, and partiality is inherently complex. Partiality fragments the world into complexity. Nature's impartiality, on the other hand, guides us back to the simplicity of Tao.

6

The Simple World vs. the Complex World

No matter what part of the world you are from, you have gone through a socialization process. This process trains you to use the razor's edge of partiality, which fragments your worldview through its tenets of names, meaning, concepts, and categories that support your perspective. In Sanskrit the word *drishti*, which means "one's perspective," is a unique way of framing the world. But all drishtis are different. The problem at the root of all drishtis is they are still views built on partiality that fragments the world.

Our consciousness is analogous to Pink Floyd's *The Dark Side of the Moon* album cover, where one pure white light is fragmented into seven colors once the one white light passes through the prism. The pure white light is the oneness of Tao, the prism is our minds, and the seven colors represent our distorted view of reality. The majority of us only live in the distorted view of the seven colors and forget their nature, and our nature *is* the pure white light of Tao. Once socialization trains us in partiality, we then create and contribute to the momentum of a complex world that our simple nature is supposed to navigate. We forget, as a result, that all we are genuinely is a localization of the one Tao expressing itself. We forget we are that one light. The result, then, is that we are molded to suit a particular drishti, and so we go through the wringer of an indoctrination process. Since we have all gone through this process, it is no wonder why we live in a complex world. We go farther and farther from the virtue of Tao when we pledge our allegiance to this process. As philosopher David Chai explains:

> Where humans go astray from the virtue of Dao lies at the moment we pledge our allegiance to names and the false reality they convey, establishing human culture as an oppositional system to the harmony of Dao.[1]

Lao-tzu and Chuang-tzu warned us. They knew if we fell for the artificial linguistic conventions and cultural frameworks, it would be hard to wrestle our awareness from these tools of partiality so that we could see the world as it indeed is. This socialization process is why human beings seem unique to the Earth and other species. We have shaped ourselves, just like Confucius wanted, and we live in a complex fantasy land rather than the natural world to which we belong. Sure, we could say that culture, language, and so on has allowed us to evolve, but it has come at the price of our health and sanity in forgetting our ultimate nature.

When we forget our nature, we believe we are what socialization drills into us (or our faces, to use Hundun as an example). Though we shouldn't be surprised about that, because this process begins from birth and only a very small minority figure out the game and begin the process of unraveling themselves from their conditioning.

Our parents were trained by the same socialization process, so they train us to prepare us for this complex reality that only exists in the mind of humanity. This is why a dog and its owner can be together, and the dog is a blank canvas in the moment while their owner is riddled with concerns and worries. I'm not suggesting we should be like dogs; however, we could learn a lot from them and other animals, as they are still connected to the natural world and know nothing of this complex reality we built in our mind. But we do, and we suffer from it.

Nevertheless, we are continually trained to label and categorize every part of reality with names and designate meaning to things. This is useful for convenience but a hindrance when we believe that world is *the* world. Society's indoctrination process wants you to believe in the artificial linguistic conventions it designed. To reinforce this programming, we are sent to school and educated in the ways of upholding and contributing to socialization. The best at memorizing and internalizing education are rewarded with more education at university. Those with the rose-colored glasses of the educated will succeed in any form of indoctrination. However, that is not true success from a Taoist perspective because most probably never realize the real world and are stuck in an illusory world.

Very few make the symbolic journey and jump on the back of an ox, like Lao-tzu, and return to the real world beyond the artificial thought structure socialization creates. Education makes sure this journey rarely if ever happens, as it continually drills into us an artificial partial system of seeing and interpreting the world. This again is not to assume education is inherently bad, but rather that it is only useful as a public utility and should never be confused for how the world truly is.

The majority of education is to serve socialization, nothing more, nothing less. It trains us to survive and function by society's rules. Once the complex reality of education is downloaded to the best of our capabilities, we are thrust into the world as an adult. As adults, we confuse the map of education through the lens of partiality with the impartial terrain of the natural world. As a result, people tend to become more fearful and political to justify their perspective over others. Actually, fear can only arise from partiality because in fragmenting our reality, we separate ourselves from the rest of the world. We measure the world according to our partial lens of education, and we become fearful of other perspectives that don't correlate with our own. Only conflict and confusion can result from living in such fear.

We essentially have different drishtis colliding. Forget about a clash of cultures, it is more like a clash of artificial linguistic frameworks. Because we all don't see the true natural world, we destroy each other and the natural world due to the complex reality we dwell in within our minds. The complex world we've been indoctrinated with is superimposed onto the natural world. As a result, we don't genuinely see the world; instead we interpret the world through the artificial linguistic conventions of partiality we've been trained with. We then live in that illusory world, dealing with those illusory problems.

Our whole life is oriented toward the upkeep of that indoctrination process. We work hard and become masters of the tenets of this complex reality so that we can climb the ladder of success to gain praise from others, which reinforces our worth to this illusory world. All that is really reinforced is one's insecurity. Our ability to be content being ourselves, being nobody, is lost in exchange for positive reinforcement from others who are suffering the same affliction. The socialization process destroys our self-esteem, as we constantly are told we are not good enough and need to succeed (whatever that means) at all costs.

In the simplicity of the natural world, we don't have any of those concerns or yearning for success because you belong as you are; you are innately secure as one with the natural world. Only the interference pattern of the partiality of socialization could distort this true reality. But we've all gone through this process, and we find it difficult to navigate life without the names, concepts, and images we've formed within our minds. We feel lost without them. The artificial, complex reality has become so much a part of us that it affects our natural feelings and inclinations.

After decades of training, we are only attracted to the artificial, complex reality because that is where we've spent the majority of our time. We find the natural world beyond the artificial linguistic framework boring. We are so accustomed to interpreting everything through our partial view and language of the world; however this is actually not the world in truth. The propensity to interpret everything according to our conditioning confuses our natural desires and needs with the framework of the artificial, complex reality. We are sporadically and mindlessly living our natural desires and inclinations through an artificial reality. Our natural desires and needs are mixed with the artificial desires and wants (not needs) of the complex reality of socialization. Lao-tzu actually addresses this problem in the Tao Te Ching. He makes a distinction between "the desires of the eye" and "the desires of the belly." He recommends that we revert back to one over the other. In chapter twelve of the Tao Te Ching, Lao-tzu explains:

> *The five colors blind our eyes.*
> *The five notes deafen our ears.*
> *The five flavors deaden our palates.*
> *The chase and the hunt madden our hearts.*
> *Precious goods impede our activities.*
> *This is why sages are for the belly and not*
> *for the eye;*
> *And so they cast off one and take up the other.*[2]

Five does have a cultural significance in ancient China. The five colors were thought of as blue, yellow, red, white, and black.

The five tones or notes of that time were C, D, E, G, and A. (This is different than Western classical music, which has seven notes.) These five notes are without B and F. The five flavors are sour, salty, sweet, spicy and bitter. Last but not least, five refers to the Five Elements Theory of *wuxing* in Traditional Chinese Medicine, which are earth, fire, water, metal, and wood. In general, then, five indicates the specific elements within a vast amount of Chinese knowledge and cultural systems. So ancient China had a tendency to divide things into five to explain something.

Five, though, is not to be seen through the same cultural lens as they used metaphorically in chapter twelve of the Tao Te Ching to explain the multitude of colors, tones, and tastes. Basically, the world of the senses. The word *five* as it appears in this chapter can easily be replaced with *extravagant* or *fancy*, because here five refers to our tendency to focus on sensual pleasures rather than moderation. The sage's advice is to go back to the desires of the belly over the desires of the eye. What are the desires of the belly and eye that Lao-tzu mentions?

THE DESIRES OF THE EYE

The desires of the eye are the things that you can see far away but you don't possess. The desires of the eye are the artificial needs created by society that keep us chasing and hunting a life that is not ours, and this, in turn, "maddens our hearts," to use Lao-tzu's words. These desires are insatiable and practically infinite. We know these desires all too well because our modern culture promotes the desires of the eye as the template for a successful life.

Think of how supposedly important Madison Avenue and the advertising industry are to modern culture. Modern advertising creates these new artificial desires through marketing. They promote the desires of the eye, and this, in turn, creates inauthentic people, which is why Lao-tzu believes these desires are dangerous. A growing swell of people, especially among the youth, will stop at nothing to be famous or have social success. But both fame and success are artificial needs planted in our mind. Striving after artificial desires suppresses our true nature. As a result, we become a soundbite generation with no depth, where we swim in the shallows. Being famous, then, becomes more important than integrity, arrogance is mistaken for humility, and marketing is more important than knowledge and wisdom.

We only have to see what nonfiction books are bestsellers and what films are the highest grossing to realize that we've built an empty culture with no depth. Granted, some few worthy books and films can get moderate exposure and reach a wider audience, but this is very rare. And last but not least, wealth is mistakenly associated with success. The symbol of success, then, is wealth, which either consciously or unconsciously motivates many people to do what they do in life. This is just the nature of a shallow culture.

In a culture driven by the desires of the eye, we get in the bad habit of trying to mimic someone else's achievements as if this is a surefire path to success. We are so often comparing our lives to others, and this breeds inauthentic people. We try to emulate other people we believe are on a pedestal. On top of this, we also try to live up to social norms that, in the end, inculcate within us a fake sincerity. This is why we feel a certain stench about some people's sincerity and their over-the-top political correctness.

Philosopher Martin Heidegger explained that when we are enacting a certain role with fake sincerity, we are driven by "they," meaning the expectations of other people and culture. As a result, we are not operating from our original nature, our deep-down raw self, minus its egotistical conditioning. Most people never encounter this raw, deep, egoless nature because most people are too busy trying to be somebody else and trying to acquire wealth. We are frequently trying to keep up with the Joneses or get ahead of them, and this attitude eclipses our true nature. As a result, we have a world that is predominately hypnotized by consumerist thinking.

Modern culture and specifically advertising sell us this idea of how our lives should be, such as the "American dream," which fuels our consumerist habits. Marketing ramps up what we think we need, but in truth, we don't need any of what they're selling. We are fooled into believing that we need the latest smartphone, car, clothes, haircut, computer, television, and whatever else is deemed trendy by advertising. We also think we need to be famous or known and respected in some way, even if, in truth, we've accomplished nothing to gain it.

These artificial desires are built on the lie that we actually need all this rubbish, but you don't need any of it. I'm going to let you in on a little secret that all these great motivational speakers of modern culture won't tell you—not everyone can have financial success or fame, and not all of us can have a brilliant idea. And you know what? None of it matters in the end because that's not why all of us are here.

We will never know why we are honestly here nor will we know our true nature if we're usually chasing our tail, and this is Lao-tzu's point. He recognized that we were so often pursuing empty desires, the desires of the eye. Keep in mind that Lao-tzu's criticisms were aimed at Confucius's carving and polishing ideology of self-cultivation, with its focus on artificial desires and an attempt to induce naturalness, which is mild compared to our modern culture.

Just imagine if Lao-tzu could see the world now; he would surely fall off his ox. Nevertheless, his advice and reaction would be the same: we need to turn our back on modern culture and return to the way of nature, the Tao. Lao-tzu's remedy for the hypnosis of the desires of the eye is to return to the natural desires of the belly.

THE DESIRES OF THE BELLY

The desires of the belly are our basic needs, what nature gave us, and are quite modest. This is quite a different picture to the Confucians who value being cultured and, as a result, become connoisseurs. But, as Lao-tzu mentioned in chapter twelve of the Tao Te Ching, having too much of anything deadens our palate. For example, instead of becoming a wine connoisseur, Lao-tzu would suggest we enjoy the wine for its own sake without becoming a wine snob.

If you are a cultured connoisseur of life, then you have moved away from simple needs. In chapter forty-six of the Tao Te Ching, Lao-tzu explains that having too many desires, like a Confucian or modern individual, is a great disaster. The Tao Te Ching states:

> *There is no greater crime than having too many desires;*
> *There is no greater disaster than not being content;*
> *There is no greater misfortune than being covetous.*[3]

In chapter forty-six, the Tao Te Ching explains that no matter our fancy explanations, excessive desires drive greed, and, in turn, greed drives aggression. As a result, we end up with the world we have now with all its conflict and tension.

If we reorient our lives toward the desires of the belly, we will realize that human beings have a simple nature and are easily satisfied. We mess with this simple nature when society creates artificial desires, and, as a result, we want more than we naturally need.

Confucian self-cultivation is about taking our raw human nature and carving and polishing it to the point that we become a superior man, *junzi* in Chinese. Lao-tzu, on the other hand, believes human nature is good, so he doesn't want you to carve or polish but instead stick to the uncarved block, as this is your simple raw nature. Confucius believed that a human should be called a "human becoming," while Lao-tzu believed that our common title of a "human being" is an accurate description because there is nothing for us to do or become. We already are naturally good, deep down. Carving and polishing contort our human nature. In chapter thirty-seven of the Tao Te Ching, it states:

Nameless unhewn wood is but freedom from desire.
Without desire and still, the world will settle itself.[4]

What chapter thirty-seven means is that if we can get back in touch with our original essence—the uncarved block—then having an urge for excessive desires will vanish. If we can just get back in touch with our original nature and forget about all of this carving and polishing, then everything will begin to order itself because our basic needs are simple. We don't have to do anything for this to happen. Instead of embarking on Confucius's journey of self-cultivation, we return home to the uncarved block. This return home encapsulates Lao-tzu's view that human perfection is through nonaction, wu-wei. Chapter forty-seven of the Tao Te Ching states:

Without going out the door, one can know the whole world.
Without looking out the window, one can see the Way of Heaven.
The further one goes, the less one knows.
This is why the sages
Know without going abroad,
Name without having to see,
Perfect through nonaction (wu-wei).[5]

Our tendency to cultivate through action driven by socialization leads to excessive desires and eclipses our true human nature. This is something skillfully explained in many Eastern spiritual traditions. All of our striving and reaching one goal after another almost never leads to contentment, but instead contributes to a world suffering from anxiety and stress, which is basically mindless and unbalanced. You surely have noticed this persistent hum of anxiety in your own life. Lao-tzu's radical advice and solution is to *know the contentment of contentment.* This is one of the greatest lines from the Tao Te Ching, and it should become a daily mantra for anyone sincere on the path of liberation. Having this unwavering contentment is something not many of us experience. It's unlikely we'll ever have this contentment if we are constantly chasing artificial desires.

The *contentment of contentment* concept is to be content with the simplicity of life. This contentment is the fundamental basics minus all modern extravagance. If you experience this contentment of contentment in your life, then you won't be drawn into the desires of the eye. Returning to the home of the uncarved block, your original, pure essence evokes this deep contentment and allows you to live a life as nature intended it. If we truly want equanimity and a sane and healthy world, then returning home to our true nature is where it all begins. To experience the contentment of contentment, we must unlearn the socialization we've endured and return to the natural desires of the belly.

THE GREAT UNDOING

One of the most famous stories in the Chuang-tzu text is about a skillful butcher known as Cook Ting or Butcher Ting (丁; Wade-Giles *Ting*; Pinyin *Ding*). There are several interpretations of this passage. The most obvious interpretation is related to the wu-wei of effortless action, or more accurately, intelligent spontaneity. The story is widely regarded as a skill story about how to be *in the zone*. This element of the story is about how to cultivate our skill so that it becomes our second nature, making our skill effortless, which gives us a sense of flow. I speak about this at length in my book *Emotional Intuition for Peak Performance*. But that is not the interpretation that addresses unlearning.

A deeper layer to the Cook Ting story relates to a great undoing. In the story, Cook Ting was cutting up oxen so effortlessly that it appeared he was in some sort of rhythmic dance or trance that allowed the ox to seamlessly fall apart in a big heap. Lord Wen-hui was very impressed with Cook Ting's skill and was eager to learn about his brilliance. Cook Ting explains:

> What I care about is the Way, which goes beyond skill. When I first began cutting up oxen, all I could see was the ox itself. After three years I no longer saw the whole ox. And now—now I go at it by spirit and don't look with my eyes. Perception and understanding have come to a stop and spirit moves where it wants. I go along with the natural makeup, strike the big hollows, guide the knife through the big openings, and follow things as they are. So I never touch the smallest ligament or tendon, much less a main joint.[6]

Cook Ting followed the movement of Tao within the ox from seeing with spirit, seeing without partiality. His knife could glide effortlessly through the makeup of the ox so that it could undo itself without any resistance. By Cook Ting following the movement of Tao, he unlocked the ox's inner potential, which then, in turn, gives nourishment to the world. The inner potential of the ox is the beef it conceals, which has the ability to nourish many people. The ox's inner potential could not have been known without the sharp blade of Cook Ting's cleaver being in harmony with the Tao. The ox was tied up in knots until Cook Ting released it from its constraints. This interpretation turns everything on its head.

In most cases, people will put themselves in the position of Cook Ting because we generally feel he represents us in our cultivation of wu-wei (and this is true from the more common interpretation). But in this deeper layer, we are the ox and Cook Ting is the Taoist sage. We are the ox tied up in the knots that socialization implanted. We were free from birth, but now our inner potential is concealed deep within because our conditioning eclipses our true nature. Cook Ting, as the Taoist sage, seeks to unlock our inner potential through a rhythmic dance that is in harmony with the Tao and unties our knots by following the path of least resistance.

The great undoing is an unlearning of the socialization process we've endured. The spiritual master attuned to the Tao is who will use their spiritual blade of impartiality to cut up your distorted view of partiality so that you can truly see again. The spiritual master or sage does not have to be a physical person; rather the Tao Te Ching or the Chuang-tzu text can be the sage that helps us undo socialization.

No matter whether it is the Tao Te Ching, Chuang-tzu, or a physical sage, we all have an inner potential that brings nourishment to the world. This inner potential is our own unique li (organic pattern) that brings harmony to the world, ying (mutual resonance and interdependence). Our li is always there, but we must let go and allow the sharp blade of wisdom to untie the knots of socialization. Once those knots are untied, our li will shine forth through simplicity and a return to our natural desires of the belly. The desires of the eye won't consume our lives because in undoing socialization, we have eradicated the fake, complex reality to see the simple world as it is.

As with Cook Ting, we must follow the path of least resistance to unlock our inner potential, our li. In this sense, the ox is actually an extension of Cook Ting, as his li (butchery) evokes ying (beef), bringing nourishment to the world. We essentially have to graduate, so to speak, from the reflection of the ox, being the student, to the actuality of Cook Ting, as the master. To be the sage we need to emulate Cook Ting. After years of training, Cook Ting follows the movement of Tao not by force, but rather by nondoing, wu-wei. He is perfectly calibrated to the environment by following the path of least resistance. Instead of hacking and sawing the ox, he glides his blade through the hollows and effortlessly undoes the ox without striking a snag. He sees the ox as a whole and so he can see into its essence.

If Cook Ting were to use his conditioned partiality, he would not be able to unlock the potential of the ox because he would see it in separate parts and so that would only lead to an effortful hacking. If we follow the path of least resistance and, as a result, harmonize with the natural movement of the Tao, then and only then will we uncover our li. We must resist our indoctrinated urge to force life to accord with our personal will. To emulate Cook Ting and undo our inner ox requires us to let go of the artificial, complicated reality of socialization and wander into the wilderness of impartiality, where simplicity is king and spontaneity is virtue.

Cook Ting's butchery was neither intentional or premeditated; rather his free and easy wandering is the spontaneous movement of universal harmony, where he is an aperture for the Tao to express itself. So his butchery and ability to unlock the potential of the ox was neither aimless or purposive. With no force, he allowed the ox to undo itself. Cook Ting evokes this great undoing because he lost his sense of self, and so his spiritual essence (li) unlocked the ox. When "we" are out of the way, the Tao functions of itself. This interpretation of the story is, in part, about how in living wu-wei we let things undo themselves in a manner best suited to one's constitution.

Each of our constitutional makeups are different and need their own processes to unlock their potential. The ox undid itself, with the guidance of Cook Ting, according to its own constitution. Cook Ting essentially allows things to undo themselves due to his harmony with the Tao. His resonance with the Tao is because the sense of self doing "something" has disappeared. All his beliefs and conditioning from the hands of social indoctrination have been eliminated. The artificial, complex reality of linguistic conventions does not disturb Cook Ting's experience. He is completely attuned to the Tao because he undid his ox to allow his inner potential (li) to come forth and bring harmony to the world (ying).

ATTUNING TO THE TAO

Cook Ting attuned himself to the Tao, where in the art of wu-wei "he" disappeared. This same attunement is available to all when we go through our own great undoing. We have to emulate Cook Ting and the reflection of the ox for any such undoing or disappearance to occur. Cook Ting allowed the world to disappear so that the Tao could make use of him. If he was consumed with daily affairs, then there was no chance for the Tao to move through him. To attune ourselves to the Tao, we must not concern ourselves with the concerns of humanity. The majority of people in the world are attuning themselves to the concerns of humanity and not the Tao. This is all due to their belief in their identities, which don't exist. Attuning oneself to the concerns of humanity indicates how one is caught in the artificial, complex reality where the superimposition of names, concepts, superficial divisions, and so on are taken to be reality. They are not.

We drastically need to return to the simple world, the way of nature. The reason why Cook Ting attuned to the Tao and undid the ox was because he unlearned the artificial, complex reality by adhering to simplicity. This process leads to true humility, the essence of Taoism. For any of us to attune ourselves to the Tao, we must unlearn the socialization that has been implanted in our mind. This cannot be done by remaining influenced by the tentacles of the artificial, elaborate reality and its linguistic conventions. We must return to simplicity. You must strip down to your mental birthday suit, so to speak, back to your original state of mind before all of this socialization.

Living a simple life is required to be attuned to the Tao. Actually, it can happen no other way, and this is why many don't know or feel the presence of Tao in their life. The Tao only gravitates toward emptiness, and to be empty in our minds requires a very simple life where you don't allow the complexity of the artificial world to infiltrate your mind. Humility is the state of consciousness that is innately residing in our pure state of consciousness. No wonder Laotzu constantly emphasized why humility is the ultimate state of the sage. We undeniably become the soft, the supple, with the ability to adapt and move with life without incurring harm on ourselves nor causing harm on others. We are an open nerve of the universe. Once we dissolve our identity by unlearning socialization, we will seek to remain in the simple world.

Keeping our mind free of mundane concerns and useless chit chat is of paramount importance. Our training of partiality can only keep our mind fixated on the illusion of separation, no matter whether they are daily concerns, conflict, or other issues. The medicine for this partiality hypnosis is simplicity, which opens the door to the true impartial world. There is no more this and that because the artificial, complex reality has been deprogrammed.

Instead of chasing our own tail in the complex reality, we stop running and return to simplicity and become the living embodiment of humility, the true person of Tao. The real attunement to Tao is realized when we finally stop the chase and the hunt and instead return to the simple living of wu-wei, where the fuel of the artificial, intricate reality has run dry.

7
The Art of Doing Nothing

Simplicity, humility, and the essential Taoist teaching of wu-wei are integral; they go hand in hand and are in essence the same. Wu-wei itself can be a confusing concept for those who are addicted to doing. A lot of Taoist teachers are also puzzled by wu-wei, as we discover through many adapting it to their own sensibilities. We need to understand wu-wei as it is. As discussed, wu-wei can be translated as effortless action, effortless living, intelligent spontaneity, noninterference, and nondoing. The essence of wu-wei is the same in all interpretations; it truly means the complete doing of nothing, hence nondoing. This concept is frightening for all those go-getters out there. But if you are interested in health and sanity, then it is the essential way of life.

Wu-wei is not just isolated to Taoism. In the Bhagavad Gita there is a Sanskrit term *nishkam karma*, which means action without the sense of doer, essentially not being attached to the fruits of your actions. We discover nishkam karma in a dialogue between Krishna and Arjuna on the battlefield of Kurukshetra. Arjuna is conflicted about fighting his cousins in the war, but Krishna urges him to fulfill his dharma (divine virtue) by becoming a limb of the Godhead (in this case Vishnu):

> To action alone hast thou a right and never at all to its fruits; let not the fruits of action be thy motive; neither let there be in thee any attachment to inaction.
>
> Fixed in yoga, do thy work, O Winner of wealth (Arjuna), abandoning attachment, with an even mind in success and failure, for evenness of mind is called yoga.[1]

The Bhagavad Gita illustrates that the complete doing of nothing is an action too. Hence, wu-wei is often translated as effortless action. This translation is primarily used in martial arts and the internal arts, for the sheer fact that once you downregulate your sense of self, then the Tao can make use of you. And this lesson of wu-wei as effortless action is one we need to abide by in our actions in the world. But if you haven't had enough sufficient training or don't understand the tenets of Taoism, then your actions will still be latent with doing, which means you are still an identity separate from the world. We cannot escape the fact that in doing, especially excessive busyness, we are still a social identity navigating the artificial, complex reality. Wu-wei in its essence as the complete doing of nothing is where the true dissolution of identity occurs. Only after that transition can our actions be purified like Arjuna's on the battlefield.

BUSYNESS STRENGTHENS
THE ILLUSION OF IDENTITY

In Taoism, Hinduism, and Buddhism, we need to pull the plug on our perpetual busyness; not just physical action, but the nonstop chatter in our minds. Zen master Thich Nhat Hanh referred to this unending noise in our head as *Radio Nonstop Thinking*, or simply Radio NST. If one is not conscious of their mind, then this radio station will deplete our energy day by day, year by year, and decade by decade.

The majority of the world is tuned into Radio NST without ever realizing how they are possessed by the activity of their mind. We are like a helpless drug addict with a chemical dependency, but our unconscious dependency is the movement of our mind that we wander with. We lack the awareness to deal with this mental addiction. We drift with our mind and confuse the incessant activity of our mind with reality. This is a kind of hypnotic sickness, which is why we see people behaving in strange ways all over the world as if being openly divisive and unnatural is somehow a virtue. This infiltration of the psyche was heightened as access to news media increased, making the mind unsteady and burdening it with concerns that are not within one's own purview. But now it has gotten even more out of hand with social media indoctrinating people and controlling their beliefs and actions through division, essentially moving them to the beat of whichever corporate drum owns the given outlet. As a result, the volume of Radio NST is off the Richter scale. It is a global addiction that we engage in mindlessly, just like fish pay no heed to the water in which they dwell. The Eastern spiritual traditions act as a medicine for this addiction. This is why in Taoism, Hinduism, and Buddhism, it is imperative to go and spend extensive time in an ashram or monastery, far away from worldly affairs and toil.

Most of us can't remain in our familiar environment and make any progress on healing ourselves from this addiction. It is extremely tiring work to engage in any deep spiritual exploration if you are still caught in the perpetual web of busyness both within and without. This is why ashrams and monasteries are typically located far away from large populations. Initially, we need to remove ourselves from society to turn off the tap of doing. Once your mind has come back to equanimity, then it is fine to return because you will be conscious of the world trying to corrupt your mind by pulling you back into the unconscious energy of busyness. If we can just give our life that space, then the tree of wu-wei will bear fruit.

We need to resist our urge to do, to act. But this does not mean that you will instantly be in wu-wei and blissed out of your mind. We are like a ceiling fan; when the fan has power, it moves very fast. However, when we turn the power off, then the fan slows down, but it takes some time for it to completely stop because of the amount of power it had. Likewise, it takes us some time to completely cease the activity of our minds because of years sprinting on the hamster wheel. We need to jump off the hamster wheel if we are to understand and embody wu-wei. We are accustomed to occupying the mind with frivolous concerns, but once the juice of doing has ceased, then a subtle tranquility begins to dawn in our mind.

So what a life away from perpetual busyness reveals is that latent within doing is identity. The more we do the more we become. Counter to this is the less we do, the less we become. We are hardly like Arjuna after receiving *satsang* (spiritual discourse direct from the master) from Krishna. We are confused and constantly occupying ourselves with busyness because of the illusion that this will define who we are. We really need to expose our motivation for doing anything. Again, this doesn't mean we shouldn't do anything, but rather our actions haven't been purified of the ego driving them, and so we cannot be karma-free from our actions without coming back to wu-wei completely.

In doing we are an identity. Our identity is the one that seeks to be active, achieve, and be successful. It is no surprise that many who become socially successful still feel a lack of fulfillment, as if they were duped into thinking they would discover the meaning of life, but all they ended up with was fool's gold. This lack of fulfillment is why many people jump from one thing to another in a perpetual cycle of doing. Our identity, which is the result of socialization, is trying to gain an ultimate fulfillment that can't be achieved by building more layers of identity due to doing. The identity needs to disappear to gain that ultimate fulfillment.

Instead of the Western idea of becoming, the Eastern path is one of being nothing, essentially nobody. Philosopher Rene Descartes once said, "I think, therefore I am." But in the East this statement is one of an identity that has separated itself from the one unified state of consciousness. There is no "I." The remedy for our madness is wu-wei. The reason why wu-wei is so effective is because when we do nothing, we vanish. The juice of doing has been cut off so the process of becoming has ceased. With wu-wei, the one who is motivated by trying to achieve this and that has disappeared.

Once we completely stop, we notice how addicted we were to doing and achieving. In completely doing nothing, there is no fuel for the identity to survive. This is why separating yourself from society or staying at an ashram or monastery is so important. When you've completely stopped, there is no oxygen for the identity to survive. The more you stifle the identity of its fuel, the less it will influence your life. The function of wu-wei is to cleanse out the socialization process we've all endured. But being nobody is frightening for most people because of the illusion of specialness and worth that socialization promotes. When you've spent enough time away from your familiar environment or spent significant time in an ashram or monastery, then you begin to understand how weak it is to try and be "somebody" special, as if you are more important than other people. You aren't, and that's a fact we will all have to live with, if we're mature enough. None of us is more important than anyone else.

Being nobody is freedom; nothing can touch you nor will you leave any trace behind. When your identity is forced to sit quietly and do nothing, it rebels and tries to hijack your awareness to engage in something, anything. Your identity is essentially what experiences boredom. By embracing boredom, we begin to put out the fire of incessant activity that downregulates the identity. Leaning into the complete doing of nothing is an act of return to the stillness of Tao (wu chi). The more we abide in wu-wei, the more we begin to emulate the emptiness of Tao. The chase and the hunt are officially over. You have become an empty vessel for the Tao to use. In the complete embodiment of wu-wei, you leave no trace.

LEAVE NO TRACE BEHIND

Wu-wei and the becoming of nothing is a central principle of Taoism, especially within the Chuang-tzu text. With wu-wei, we dissolve the identity, which allows us to live in harmony with the Tao. Living wu-wei, then, evokes our true nature of oneness. But the problem is when we are addicted to doing, hence being a separate identity, this reality of oneness is eclipsed. Chuang-tzu explains that it is by doing nothing that our nature is restored:

> There was a man who, frightened
> by his shadow and disgusted with
> his footprints, tried to outrun them.
> However, the more he raised his feet, the
> more footprints he left behind. He ran
> faster and faster but his shadow would
> not leave him. Believing he was too
> slow, he ran faster still, without pause,
> exhausting his strength and dying. He did
> not know that by staying in the shade his
> shadow would have vanished, and that by
> resting peacefully any trace of him would
> cease. How utterly foolish he was![2]

Leave behind no trace, no shadow, no footprints. You essentially never were here in reality. The idea of your identity is a fabrication. As Chuang-tzu stated, by doing nothing and resting in the shade, any trace of his sense of self would cease. This is the act of wu-wei. This is the beauty of Taoism. But from the perspective of social-ization this is complete nonsense because you ought to be someone so that the social machine and the hypnosis of the masses can con-tinue unfettered. Socialization itself is designed to create isolated individuals that serve the machine, even though many individuals believe they are free. Indeed they are not free; no matter whether it is democracy, communism, or fascism, you are still a product of a socialization process and that indoctrination obscures your vision of reality as it truly is. We definitely could say there are degrees to the oppression we subtly feel from authoritarian sociopolitical ideolo-gies, but the fact is none coincide with the way of nature, and so the oppression is there either subtle or gross.

Once socialization has duped people into walking away from their original face of the traceless, they live with a mentality of try-ing to leave a trace, the biggest footprint they can make. The Taoist view of leaving no trace behind makes many people nervous and confused because the proponents of socialization are often beating the drum of personal success and heightened individuality, par-ticularly in the West. Instead of the wu-wei process that thins our identity away, most feel we need to invest in it and make it shine according to socialization. But all that happens by trying to make it shine is differing degrees of suffering, but suffering, nevertheless. The accepted way of leaving the biggest footprint behind only causes you harm and harm to others.

Trying to be an identity, and the most prevalent identity, is exhausting. The chase and the hunt kill our innocence slowly but surely. We are anxiously trying to establish our identities, our worth, and the irony is that the identity itself is a ghost. This is why

Chuang-tzu said it was utterly foolish. If only the masses knew that by resting in the shade, their shadow would disappear, erasing all trace of self. What freedom that is. But this freedom is obscured by the chase and the hunt we are all on.

It is common for people indoctrinated by the socialization process to speak about how important legacy is to them. We particularly hear athletes and artists in the modern day speak about their legacy, as if they are important, not only now but for future generations. I always cringe when I hear such arrogance. Some people genuinely believe they will be remembered like the Buddha. Trust me; they almost surely won't. The majority of souls who have lived on this planet left no trace behind. They might have been anxiously trying to leave the biggest footprint like many today, but the reality is that you likely won't be remembered in time. This realization should be liberating, but it scares most people, especially those hunting a legacy.

You must be "somebody" at all costs because that guarantees success, whatever that means. You must not be "nobody" because that means you're a loser. This mentality is ass-backward. In rubbing out your footprints and resting in the shade, you are finally secure in being nobody, your original face. Trying to be somebody proves how insecure we are to just be as we are. In psychology they speak about how our yearning for social success exposes a lack of self-esteem. We suffer from self-esteem issues, and so we want to gain it by becoming successful by any means necessary. The only problem is that when we attain that success, the same self-esteem issues remain. The reason for this is because inherent within the identity is a low self-esteem. A low self-esteem is within the identity because the identity is isolated from the rest of the world, and so it is under the illusion it doesn't belong. What a true delusional trip we impose on ourselves.

The fact of the matter is you do belong; you can only belong, but to understand that you need to leave no trace by living wu-wei. Chasing a legacy proves that you are under the impression you don't belong. The fact is that those who are hunting a legacy have low self-esteem and are actually weak. All throughout history we've had numerous examples, especially world leaders and tyrants (if the two can be separated). The tyrant is the weakest individual, and, as a result, they project their low self-esteem on the world.

Tyrannical rulers can only come about because of their inability to rest in the shade, eliminating any trace of themselves. They must leave the biggest trace, and this unfortunately has become the mindset of the masses. We are often, then, one step away from becoming a tyrant. That is the tricky terrain we all traverse when we are after a legacy. Chasing the legacy burns us out, and, as a result, your legacy is only relevant to you and only exists in your mind. The world wants you to be a go-getter, but you deplete your energy in the process, which reduces your vitality and lifespan.

In living wu-wei, we rest in the shade of the tree to rejuvenate our spirit, which allows us to absorb the Tao's nourishment, leading to longevity. In taking it easy and not striving, we replenish our spirit. This is the key for health, sanity, and an equanimous mind. Too much effort stresses our mind and body. Life is not a rush. Take it easy and harmonize with the graceful rhythm of Tao. You will only burn yourself out and reduce your lifespan from trying to leave a trace, a legacy. There is really no upside. We just have to come to our senses and understand that in doing nothing, all is truly done because we all belong to the Tao and are *it*.

Astonishingly, we forget the Tao due to thousands of years of incessant effort in trying to be "somebody." We invested in the shadow of our true nature, which, as Chuang-tzu points out, doesn't exist when we are resting in the shade. We built a scaffolding of ourselves in our mind, a self-image, that doesn't exist. We forget our original face and the Tao in the process. But it is not the Tao we should have forgotten; it is this illusion of self that should and will be forgotten when we leave no trace.

FORGET YOURSELF, FORGET THE WORLD

Socialization creates an elaborate cultural framework for us to download—linguistic, religious, social, and political. We live through this framework and so we don't see the world as it clearly is, but rather how we've been trained to see it. Living wu-wei, on the other hand, deconstructs this artificial framework by leaving no trace. This is done by a forgetting of the socialization we've been indoctrinated with instead of the Tao. The way social assimilation is forgotten is because when we stop doing and leave no trace, this affects the identity at a root level where we begin to drop the artificial linguistic conventions we've been indoctrinated by. What happens, then, is we naturally forget the qing's disposition of dissecting the world into this and that, right and wrong, and so on. In forgetting right and wrong, we can see the world again.

A complete forgetting of the self is required to see the real oneness of life. Forgetting the qing cleanses our vision to see wholeness. The more we chip away or downregulate this sense of self, the more seeing the world as Chuang-tzu did will be achieved. At the fundamental level, in living wu-wei, we forget the sense of self because the illusion of separation (maya) has evaporated. Once separation is forgotten, "you" have vanished. Oneness and wholeness are your reality when separation and its child of identity have disappeared. The mind becomes still and naturally comfortable in a state of oneness. The natural state of the mind after all is empty, spontaneous, and free, so oneness is its reality. That is, until we fill it full of socialization and the habit of qing.

Being settled in reality as it genuinely is enables our mind to be present and act spontaneously with no components of separation influencing our actions. We are like the zhenren, a genuine person, flowing with life like a leaf down a mountain stream, as Chuang-tzu implores us to "ride along with things and allow your heart-mind to wander. Entrust yourself to the inevitable and nourish that which lies central within—this is perfection."[3]

No conditioned mind could allow the heart-mind to wander effortlessly. We must forget ourselves to allow Tao to use us as it will. To embody the forgetting, Chuang-tzu recommends a nondiscriminating and intuitive way to engage with the world (as discussed throughout this book). When there is no identity interfering with the reality we experience, we act immediately and appropriately to life as life itself. We are, as a result, perfectly calibrated to the world. All conditioning of separation has vanished, so one doesn't discriminate and cut up the reality based on their identity. Our intuition, then, functions as a limb of Tao, where it is immediate and appropriate in a way that would make Zen masters extremely happy.

It is ironic that when we believe we are the person we've been trained to become, our intuition suffers. Our identity acts as an interference pattern to intuition. We cannot act naturally with our intuition fully charged because our acting and intuition are filtered through our conditioned identity. As a result, we cannot act and react authentically. All conflict and confusion arise from filtering reality through our conditioned identity. What trouble could there be if we had no conditioning? That's right, none. We would see reality in its true oneness. With a nondiscriminating and naturally intuitive mind, we see reality beyond names, images, and meaning.

In forgetting ourselves, the artificial linguistic conventions are torn down. As a result, your intuition is harmonized with the world because you are one with the world. You move as one with the river of Tao. Once the program of reality has been erased, you merge with Tao and experience reality as a whole. The art of forgetting is a two-sided coin, on one side you forget the self and live in harmony with the Tao, and on the other side, the side most people exist on, you forget the Tao and live in an illusion of separation filtered through your conditioned identity. When we forget the Tao, all hell breaks loose.

Suffering is the standard state of consciousness in a Taoless reality. But our true nature can never suffer because it doesn't live through a hollow world of names, images, and meaning. We may forget the Tao, but the sage never does. The sage forgets socialization, identity, and ultimately the program they unwillingly downloaded. In forgetting what is false, their selfless virtue reverberates through the consciousness of humanity. We, too, are a sage at heart, but we forget what is real, the Tao. Chuang-tzu explains the forgetfulness of both sides of the coin:

> *Thus if one's virtue endures, appearances can be forgotten. When men do not forget the things they ought to forget, and forget the things they should not forget, this is a case of forgetting that which is real.[4]*

Forgetting what is real is called *chengwang* in Chinese (誠忘: Wade-Giles *ch'eng-wang*; Pinyin *chengwang*). The sage never falls victim to chengwang because all appearances have been forgotten. Forgetting the appearance or superimposition on the world is also a teaching within Advaita Vedanta. In Sanskrit there is the famous phrase *Brahma Satyam Jagat Mithya*, which means "Brahman alone is the only reality/truth, the world is an appearance." To articulate this knowledge, Advaita Vedanta uses the snake and rope as an analogy. All that exists is the rope. But when we perceive reality through our identity then we believe the rope is a snake, and we act accordingly. We begin to live in fear because we don't see reality as it truly is as the rope. We are fooled by the appearance, but the appearance only exists in our mind.

People sometimes say "what you see is what you get," but this statement is inaccurate because what you see is how you've been trained to interpret what you see. If it were indeed "what you see is what you get," then that statement would be referring to the splendor of oneness, the Tao. The sage never forgets that statement in its truest context. Having merged with the river, they could never forget because the Tao lives through them. They are never hindered by the identity and socialization process. The sage is in harmony with the Tao because they are a living embodiment of wu-wei. They forget the self, and so they dwell in the real world beyond distinction.

The sage does not cling to fears or desires, and so the events of life cannot make their mind gallop here and there. Most people, though, wander millions of miles daily in their mind. Once your activity of mind (*vrittis* in Sanskrit) has consumed your life, it is impossible to remember the Tao, your true nature. Only in settling the whirlpools of mind can you engage with the Tao.

The mind's essence is a reflection of Tao, and its nature is empty, spontaneous, and free. To experience the nature of reality requires us to forget ourselves and fast the activity from our mind. This is why in many spiritual practices in the East, stillness is a complete state of nothingness or emptiness, the heart of wu-wei. Once the whirlpools of the mind settle, we can see into our true nature, which is tranquil and undisturbed. The stillness of the mind is so complete within the sage that they embody the Tao. They truly have no sense of self within, even though they function as a normal human in daily life. Once we forget the identity, then our perception begins to transform, or more correctly, begins to come back to its original state of awareness. We then live in a world completely different from the masses.

Oneness is our house, to use Chuang-tzu's words. There is no more this and that, only the wholeness of Tao. This begins to change our interaction with reality, as eleventh-century literary genius Wang Pang explains in his commentary on the Chuang-tzu:

> *The sage embodies Dao and is thus*
> *without a relational-self. Being selfless,*
> *there is nothing in him to oppose the*
> *world. . . . There is not a thing that is*
> *without its opposite and Dao alone in its*
> *marvelousness is unequaled. Being without*
> *equal and returning to the One, one can*
> *forget the difference between self and*
> *other. This is the equality of things.*[5]

There is no more self and other once we embody Tao. The oneness of life is discovered in forgetting ourselves. Our perception and felt experience begin to harmonize with oneness as a result.

SEEING TAO IN ALL

The illusion of separation is eliminated from the sage's mind. The sage sees the Tao in all as Chuang-tzu stated by "seeing the infinite in all things." He had to reside in the still point of the Tao beyond this and that to witness the true reality of oneness. Once the sage's perception is cleansed of separation, then they can see the Tao in all and all in Tao. The sage, then, sees the true nature of all beings as identical to their own being, as there surely is no separation. This evolution of perception is commonly verified by spiritual masters throughout the ages. In the nondual path of Advaita Vedanta, one of the aspirants' perceptual effects of abiding in their true Self (Atman) is that they see the Atman in all because Atman is identical with Brahman. As the great twentieth-century sage Ramana Maharshi said, "For a realised being sees only the Self, just like a goldsmith estimating the gold in various items of jewellery sees only gold."[6]

Atman is all there truly is. Anything else we can conceive of is maya, or in other words, a product of qing. The great Ramana

Maharshi is the perfect example of a modern-day sage who saw the Atman or Tao in all. Arising from that divine intuitive sense, he had immense wisdom, compassion, empathy, and forgiveness because, from abiding in the Atman, his intrinsic natural qualities were amplified. Ramana's world is a possibility for all of us, depending on how radical we are willing to be.

To enhance your perception so that you are grounded in the ultimate reality of Brahman (Tao), there are a lot of spiritual practices you need to engage in. One specific practice in relation to seeing the Atman in all is the recitation of the phrase "All is Brahman, and I am That." This specific phrase is meant to be a walking meditation. It is designed to get you out of your qing and subtly train your awareness to see reality as it truly is. After some training, your mind will loosen its grip on labeling and interpreting everything it sees. You will live with true ease and won't be hindered by your mind.

When your sense of identity disappears, you truly know all is Brahman, all is Tao. As a result, the sage sees the tzu-jan ("naturalness" or "self-evident nature") of the myriad things (ten thousand things). They can witness the natural harmony and beauty of life, which surely is splendid and not the dark and confused reality most assume life to be. Witnessing the true oneness of life is due to the "I" disappearing. To forget oneself is to lose oneself, and this is extremely important because the presence of "I" diminishes the Tao within our being.

A great silence overcomes our mind once we firmly abide in our true nature. There is no noise in the mind, and we genuinely see the Tao in all, not as a separate entity, but rather as one with everything. This silence we live in resulting from forgetting oneself and seeing the Tao in all is the complete embodiment of wu-wei. This state of consciousness is the real comfortable station in our life. We are in the living embrace of Tao. We forget about the notions of competition, deceit, praise, honor, and so on. This deafening silence is the representation of the natural emptiness of Tao within our being.

Tao gathers in emptiness. This is where *qi* flows (氣: Wade-Giles *ch'i*; Pinyin *qi*). Once all blockages are removed, qi flows effortlessly. A great example of this process is Yen Hui from the fasting the mind passage of the Chuang-tzu text. All throughout the story, Yen Hui is going through a process of self-forgetting. In his case, he is forgetting to be a sage. Confucius, as the mouthpiece of Chuang-tzu in the story, continually scolds Yen Hui's attempts to change a tyrannical ruler in the state of Wei. As a result, Yen Hui engages himself in a form of self-reductionism. He begins to peel away the layers of conditioning, starting with the socialization program of Confucianism, then the body, until he reaches total self-forgetting. This is the meaning behind Chuang-tzu's phrase "sit in forgetfulness." Having embodied this forgetfulness, Yen Hui is an empty vessel living in silence. Now the Tao can make use of him.

In silence we receive the qi of Tao. Just as the hollows of the trees receive the qi of wind, so do we receive the qi of Tao when our internal landscape has become silent. In the silence of living wu-wei, Yen Hui could make oneness his house, as Chuang-tzu put it. He can now see the Tao in all because from silence, his awareness has returned to its true, pure state. Yen Hui has become natural again, and this is the great possibility for all of us. In following wu-wei, we forget ourselves, leaving no trace behind. As a result, we begin to live in reality as it truly is, which is completely different to the reality of the masses.

8

The Spontaneous Reality

The real world of the Tao is a spontaneous reality. The sage lives in this spontaneous reality. The Taoist concept of tzu-jan is alluding to the natural world being spontaneously of itself. This means precisely of itself and not filtered through a medium of some sort. This may be hard for many of us to fathom because we often frame our experience through a language bound by concepts, beliefs, and meanings. Nature is the best example because it is the embodiment of tzu-jan regardless of how we interpret it. Our mind is, too, like nature, but we pollute it full of garbage that we take on as our identity.

The mind's essence is empty, spontaneous, and free until socialization steps in. Social and cultural indoctrination warps the innate spontaneity of the mind. This process destabilizes the way we think and how we experience reality. Our mind, as a result, is trained to think in a linear fashion, but that is completely out of sync with the spontaneous reality.

THE ILLUSION OF THINKING

Understanding and living within the spontaneous reality depends on our awareness of how thoughts function according to the Eastern spiritual traditions. There are two layers to this; one is how linear thinking and thoughts create the ego, and the second, deeper layer is about thinking without language, which I will dissect in the section starting on page 174. Let's tackle the first layer; why do thoughts create the illusion of self?

We all think, and thoughts persist. No matter whether you're a sage or an average joe, the stream of consciousness is continuous. Beware of any sages or gurus or spiritual masters who claim they have no thoughts. Thoughts obviously persist for everyone. But the way the sage experiences thoughts is completely different to us because they dwell in the spontaneous reality. Their different relationship with thoughts is why they have no strong sense of self, which will become self-evident as we go on.

Thoughts are typically believed to be linear, creating a continuity of thinking that our awareness wanders with. Each thought depends on the next, creating this linkage or chain of thoughts. This is a common experience for most of us. But is it actually the nature of thoughts and thinking?

In Eastern spiritual traditions, thoughts are not assumed to be linear, not a one-after-the-other process. As with anything in nature, thoughts grow of themselves. They, too, are a product of tzu-jan. Taoism, like many other Eastern spiritual traditions, is a tradition grounded in nonduality, and so instead of a linear-based thinking system as part of a world of separation, Taoism is based on nondual thoughts and nondual thinking because reality is fundamentally spontaneous, not separate and isolated.

The Eastern spiritual model reveals that thoughts exist one at a time and not as a continuation of thoughts as we commonly believe. They grow spontaneously and don't depend on the next thought. Zen teacher David Loy calls this natural thought the *unsupported thought*, as thoughts are inherently unsupported. Thoughts, then, are not the problem. The real problem is when thoughts begin to link with other thoughts that follow (a common experience for most of us). For example, think of a typical chain—each link is a thought. When those links connect, we have a chain of thinking. This continuity of thoughts (the chain) creates an illusion of self. We then experience reality through hardwired ways of thinking based on our past experiences and memory. But everything is always new, no matter how familiar the experience may feel. We often fall victim to this unconscious habit.

We will experience something in the present that our subconscious recognizes as having some similarity with a past event, and then we react with the same emotion, even though the new experience in reality has no connection to the past. The Eastern psychological framework of Samsara (Wheel of Samsara) contributes to this habit of linking thoughts. This framework is primarily based on how memory hinders our experience in the present. The inner layer of the Wheel of Samsara framework is *samskaras*, which is a Sanskrit word meaning mental impressions and subliminal psychological imprints. Basically, samskaras are the subconscious. The next layer is *vasanas*, a Sanskrit word meaning habitual ways and latent tendencies. The outer layer is *karma*, Sanskrit for actions and unconscious actions.

In brief, the samskaras stimulate the vasanas, and our vasanas mobilize our karma to act. In other words, our subconscious fuels our habits and tendencies, and those hardwired habits make us act and react in predictable ways. This framework reveals why we emotionally react to familiar experiences because it is all the result of having a full storehouse of impressions within the samskaras. The reason why this psychological framework is related to Samsara is that this cycle is what keeps us coming back, life after life, to experience the same patterns within our daily life. Those samskaras contribute to the common habit of linking thoughts, because when these samskaras influence our vasanas, we follow a predictable chain of thoughts according to our subconscious.

Basing our present experience on past experiences is all due to the samskaras. This is why, as discussed, fasting the mind is imperative to clean out this storehouse consciousness so that we can experience the spontaneous beauty of reality. But we are trained to live in an unnatural world, and our thinking reflects that. We believe that each thought is related to the next, so we drag that out, creating this illusion of self. The linkage of thoughts is based on the illusion that each thought is supported by the next. But, according to the Eastern spiritual traditions, a thought is naturally unsupported when it is not dependent upon anything else. There essentially is no chain. Thoughts bubble up spontaneously, independent until we link them with our clumsy wandering mind.

The true nature of thoughts is that they don't arise from each other. The links are in fact not connected. The unsupported thought arises nondually. This spontaneous unsupported thought, then, is the Buddhist wisdom of *prajna*, which means nondual knowledge and wisdom. When thoughts are not linking up in a series, but instead flowering spontaneously and nondually, this is prajna. Philosopher and scholar Daisetsu Teitaro Suzuki explains the unsupported thought with the concept prajna:

> It is important to note here that *prajna* wants to see its diction "quickly" apprehended, giving us no intervening moment for reflection or analysis or interpretation. *Prajna* for this reason is frequently likened to a flash of lightning or a spark from two striking pieces of flint. "Quickness" does not refer to progress of time; it means immediacy, absence of deliberation, no allowance for an intervening proposition, no passing from premises to conclusion.[1]

Thoughts then spring up independently and are not supported by the next. This understanding of the unsupported thought is an inspiration behind the development of koans in Zen Buddhism and the martial arts of Taoism. A koan, for example, is a riddle, sometimes completely illogical, that the master asks the disciple. The master is expecting an immediate response. The disciple is criticized for hesitation and praised for their apparently nonsensical but immediate reply (eventually the disciple's response ought to be appropriate, which is a higher level of training).

Hesitation itself indicates a logical train of thought. In other words, hesitation is a self-conscious paralysis of thought that handicaps your ability to experience reality spontaneously. When most of us are presented with a question, no matter how silly, we experience this self-conscious paralysis of thought. We overthink and overanalyze. Hesitation is an obstacle we must overcome to live in the spontaneous reality. To eliminate hesitation and dwell in the unsupported thought, we need to ask what causes the linkage of thoughts?

MIND SEEKING

In truth our mind lacks nothing. Its nature is empty, spontaneous, and free. However, our mind links thoughts together, which is enhanced by how we are trained to interact with the world. Why would the mind try to fix itself? The Buddha resolved this conundrum twenty-five hundred years ago through the revelation of the Second Noble Truth. The cause of suffering is craving. That is the Second Noble Truth. Buddha was not really speaking about physical or psychological desires per se, but rather he was speaking about seeking itself. Why does the mind seek or crave?

The mind tries to objectify itself because it is uncomfortable with its own emptiness and formlessness. With no understanding of the mind, we unconsciously fall into this ingrained habit of seeking. As a result, the mind tries to fix itself to find a secure home. Our experience in the external world and with the socialization process diminishes our resonance with the mind's empty disposition. We incorrectly feel we lack with our emptiness, and so we try to fill this bottomless hole. We can never fill the mind up because its nature is formless and empty.

The socialization process leans into the mind's habit to seek. With all of the social and cultural training, we feel we need to validate our existence by becoming an identity. The process of becoming somebody, then, is self-defeating because our obsession with gaining and proving something keeps the mind from its own empty nature. The sense of identity or ego, then, is a process that continually attempts to secure itself. It is trying to construct a permanent home within the mind, but the problem is the foundation of the house is empty. No matter how much concrete we pour into the foundation, the mind remains intrinsically empty. The ego, as a result, tries to deny its emptiness and becomes restless in chasing and grasping the next thought, hence the ego is constantly thrust into the future and never resides totally in the present moment. This whole mindless process is caused by the nature of mind seeking, which the Buddha explained.

So the mind has an inherent flaw because it continually thinks its fundamental task is to find and dwell in a secure home for itself, as if it is homeless. We are just not comfortable with the natural empty home we inherited from nature, so we feel we need to renovate. But this renovation is a dead end. Zen master Hui Hai suggests we need to return to the nature of our true nondwelling home and cease the search for dwelling:

> Should your mind wander away, do not follow it, whereupon your wandering mind will stop wandering of its own accord. Should your mind desire to linger somewhere, do not follow it and do not dwell there, whereupon your mind's questing for a dwelling-place will cease of its own accord. Thereby, you

will come to possess a non-dwelling mind—a mind which remains in the state of non-dwelling. If you are fully aware in yourself of a non-dwelling mind, you will discover that there is just the fact of dwelling, with nothing to dwell upon or not to dwell upon. This full awareness in yourself of a mind dwelling upon nothing is known as having a clear perception of your own nature. A mind which dwells upon nothing is the Buddha-Mind, the mind of one already delivered, Bodhi-Mind, Uncreate Mind . . . you will have attained to understanding from within yourself—an understanding stemming from a mind that abides nowhere, by which we mean a mind free from delusion and reality alike.[2]

The mind's flawed habit of seeking and its identification and obsession with various types of phenomena hold it back from realizing its nondwelling nature of emptiness and formlessness. This error in awareness within the mind is the reason why, when the mind wants something and obtains it, it quickly moves to something else it believes it wants. We've all experienced this, and this is what keeps alive the terrible habit of consumerism. But this state of seeking can never fulfill itself, and this is why when we obtain the next desire, we feel as empty as ever. The reason for this is, in truth, the mind wants itself, its true empty and formless disposition, but the linkage of thoughts eclipses this from happening. As a result of this process, as discussed, the mind tries to grasp itself, creating the ego. This gives an artificial security, but there is a price to pay because fear is generated at the same time, as anything grasped that we become attached to can and often will be lost. Hence our fear of physical death and the death of the ego.

No matter how hard we try to hold on to our ego at the time of physical death, we are forced finally to let go. Taoism, and Eastern spirituality in general, are technologies designed to avoid procrastination and, instead, kill the ego now so that we can truly live. The socialization process that colors and conditions the ego must be cleansed out of our being. Once the conditioning is gone, it is hard for the ego to survive. But only the sincerest spiritual aspirants embark upon this process because most people can't face the fact that all things pass, and this includes the death of this artificial construct in our mind, the ego or identity.

The death of the ego becomes a suffering that pervades our lives, both consciously and unconsciously. In some sense, we can accept the death of our body, but the death of the ego we've become is frightening. But this death, or at least a significant downregulation of the ego, is required to penetrate and abide in the true spontaneous reality. How do we cease the linkage of thoughts so that the unsupported thought can grow spontaneously of itself?

MEDITATION AS SPIRITUAL SOLVENT

The natural corrective to the linkage of thoughts is meditation. And I don't mean any piecemeal meditations but instead strict lengthy meditation practices on a daily basis. Deep meditation is the remedy. Such traditional practices as Vichara (self-inquiry) in Advaita Vedanta, open awareness (zazen) in Zen Buddhism, Dzogchen in Vajrayana Buddhism, and Vipassana in Theravada Buddhism are great remedies for our hypnosis because they have a profound effect on our character and calm, leading to true equanimity. Consistent daily meditation with such methods has a massive impact on the mind. You essentially are retraining your mind to function naturally and spontaneously as it is designed. The way meditation achieves this is its natural function, whether we know it or not, and is a process of letting go of thoughts, which breaks up the habitual linking of thoughts into a series.

With an attuned awareness, we isolate each thought without following the next one. We often fail at this because the mind tends to wander. But with patience and perseverance, you begin to notice each thought unsupported by the next, and so you begin to end the continuity of thoughts, which is how the ego begins to die. This is why the wandering mind is a central focus in meditation. Once we break the links of the chain, we free ourselves to be who we truly are. The chain of thoughts is what imprisons us: meditation, on the other hand, sets us free.

Meditation acts as a spiritual solvent for our sticky minds. Our awareness can see thoughts naturally arising of themselves, and we don't follow the next thought, nor do we identify the thought with a memory. They just drift by like clouds on a clear blue sky. Zen master Huang Po explained this when he wondered why his students would not let go of thoughts, since this letting go breaks up the linkage of thoughts: "Why do they [students of Zen] not copy me by letting each thought go as though it were nothing, or as though it were a piece of rotten wood, a stone, or the cold ashes of a dead fire?"[3]

Traditional forms of meditation bring us back to our natural mind, which is empty, spontaneous, and free. Our thinking is essentially nondual, and this is why in Zen Buddhism, they developed koans. Koans test the student's mind to see if there is hesitation or immediacy. But this is taken a step further in Zen through prajna. Prajna implies spontaneous nondual wisdom or knowledge in other words. So instead of just being immediate, the ultimate state of mind is to be both immediate and appropriate to each and every situation. This state is in harmony with the spontaneous reality and is the end objective of both Zen koan and martial arts training. You essentially function as a limb of Tao.

Reasoning, then, is not necessary for choosing the appropriate response. What arises spontaneously in the mind will be appropriate if self-hesitation does not interfere. This is prajna, an unpolluted intuitive way of thinking that is nondual. The sage operates from this state of prajna intuition. They dwell in a spontaneous reality that is a mirror of their mind: empty, spontaneous, and free. They abide in the second, deeper layer of the spontaneous reality, where thoughts have no color or context.

THOUGHTS WITHOUT LANGUAGE

Once we get beyond the illusion of the linkage of thoughts to the unsupported thought, we notice that thoughts of themselves are conditioned by language. This may sound like an odd question, but what would thoughts be without the linguistic framework we've been trained with? If there were no language, would thoughts exist? This is definitely something most people have never contemplated. What does a naked thought feel like? Why are thoughts formed the way they are through language?

These questions can be addressed with the first layer of the spontaneous reality because when we go beyond the linkage of thoughts and our language-laced thoughts infecting our immediate reality, we are left with prajna. Thoughts do arise, then, without language, but they grow spontaneously of themselves, tzu-jan. A thought's self-evident nature is prajna intuition, a feeling not stained by language-infused emotions or thoughts. However, the spontaneous nature of thoughts devoid of language is something profoundly beyond words or explanation because there aren't many words other than Tao, Brahman, and Dharmakaya to describe the real world beyond artificial linguistic conventions.

The reality of Tao is truly beyond words, even though we use the word *Tao* to clumsily refer to it (this is the benefit of words). When something is breathtaking or inexplicable, we often say "I have no words to describe it." The words vanish, and what we are left with is awe, an awe spawned from the innate oneness of the spontaneous reality. However, even though we have no words, we feel the experience, and the thoughts are linked to our feelings and not a language to describe the feeling. In a great piece of art there is a beauty that is indescribable, and this is the same for the beauty of life.

When you are attuned to the Tao you can feel and sense this oneness, which quite frankly, will overwhelm you with joy. This oneness is the ground of being. In this space, thoughts are naked, not infused with beliefs, concepts, or identity. They arise just as an intuitive feeling because nature is fundamentally spontaneous, so our thinking is, in reality, nondual. This intuitive way of thinking is the intelligent spontaneity aspect of wu-wei. Essentially, you are what the Zen master or Taoist martial arts practitioner want you to become, a living embodiment of nature. The irony is that we are that unpolluted nature from birth until the world steps in with their carving and polishing model of cultivation.

Prajna intuition, on the other hand, is how we act immediately and appropriately to all life because we are perfectly calibrated to life, to the Tao. We are moving efficaciously as an unpolluted limb of life. Our lives are harmoniously aligned with the way of the Tao. No thought infused with language or identity could distort our experience. Once our actions and reactions are not determined by thoughts infected by language and identity (not to mention the linkage), then our thinking becomes naturally prajna intuition. This nondual intuitive thinking is a spontaneous feeling in harmony with the world, minus emotions and linguistic framework. These unsupported thoughts have no color, and so they are buck naked as nature intended.

As discussed, it is extremely rare to inquire about the nature of thoughts before our language shaped our thinking. But these are the mysterious depths Taoism and Eastern spirituality like to explore. With no socialization, no identity, no linkage of thoughts, and no language, our thoughts are intuitive responses in harmony with the environment. Not to mention, there are no worries without all of this programming. However, words and language themselves won't evaporate from your mind, and this is not a problem per se. The difference between the sage and you and I is the sage doesn't confuse his learned language for the experience of reality. They live from prajna intuition, and so language has been demoted to a public utility.

Language itself is a wonderful development in culture and is very useful as a public utility, great for interaction and sharing knowledge and ideas. For example, I am able to discuss the Tao with you in this book, which is amazing. But the problem is when we believe the map is the territory. The map or language is useful in gaining knowledge about the territory or spontaneous reality or Tao, but it can never *be* that. One must go through the process of return (wu chi) and step into the indescribable natural world beyond words.

THE SPONTANEOUS NATURAL WORLD

There is no more division once we abide in the ground of being, Atman. All division is a construct of socialization, language, identity, and people with self-interested agendas who are delusional. All that there is in the real world is oneness, no form of separation, because separation is the illusion of maya or qing. Even though this is the truth, some will do anything to avoid the real world. Many people still have an axe to grind based on their identity and its subjective biases. The classic four pillars of separation of religion, nation, race, and sex are used, plus their derivatives. But those who fervently believe they are fundamentally any of these pillars and their subdivisions are actually the same as what they oppose because believing in any of these illusions as if they are fundamentally real is innately divisive. They are all an illusion and don't exist in the real world of the spontaneous reality of Tao.

When separation is gone, what is left is an unassociated love arising from oneness. This is a deep love not determined by individual association and biases. It is a love that is innate within our being, transcending all words to describe it. It is an unassociated love belonging to the spontaneous reality. Naturally, as a result of this unassociated love, compassion, forgiveness, empathy, and humility are amplified intrinsic qualities that are part of the felt experience of prajna intuition. We are in harmony with the spontaneous reality.

The soft stillness of nature becomes our disposition, and that is how we respond to life. This is the embodiment of embracing the yin energy of Tao. The real soft overcoming the illusory hard. But this softness is not favorable in a world full of competition, aggression, and hate. Nevertheless, the softness of nature is the essence of the emptiness of Tao. Humility, for example, as discussed, is thought to be useless. But in truth it is where true power resides. Without the apparent uselessness of humility, compassion, and forgiveness, all the emotional fires raging in the world would not be put out. Actually, the world hypnotically believes that adding more fuel to the fire will resolve the issue. This will never be possible.

What we incorrectly assume to be useless is, in truth, what brings peace and equanimity into the hearts and minds of all. And the useless soft stillness of nature is wu-wei. So humility, compassion, and forgiveness are intrinsic qualities of wu-wei. In the end, nothing is more useless than wu-wei. Chuang-tzu explains this beautifully in the useless tree story. The useless tree is actually a symbol of wu-wei. In the story people scoff at the uselessness of the contorted useless tree. What use does it have? They can't make anything out of it. But what they don't see is that the useless tree loves and nourishes all without lording it over them. The useless tree lives for itself without interfering in the lives of others. As a result, the useless tree contributes to the benefit of others without intending to do so. The story states:

Tzu-ch'i of Nan-po was wandering
around the Hill of Shang when he saw a
huge tree there, different from all the
rest. A thousand teams of horses could
have taken shelter under it and its shade
would have covered them all. Tzu-ch'i
said, "What tree is this? It must certainly
have some extraordinary usefulness!"
But, looking up, he saw that the smaller
limbs were gnarled and twisted, unfit for
beams or rafters, and looking down, he
saw that the trunk was pitted and rotten
and could not be used for coffins. He
licked one of the leaves and it blistered
his mouth and made it sore. He sniffed
the odor and it was enough to make a
man drunk for three days. "It turns out
to be a completely unusable tree," said
Tzu-ch'i, "and so it has been able to grow
this big. Aha!—it is this unusableness that
the Holy Man makes use of!"[4]

The useless tree is perfectly calibrated to the Tao and this in turn is transmitted to other beings. It achieves such union and unintended virtue by being a living embodiment of wu-wei. The uselessness of the useless tree is natural. The useless tree is a metaphor for the Taoist sage. Many people believe the sage's knowledge and wisdom is useless, yet they are drawn to their enlightened presence. Something about the sage brings comfort, even to the most hardened heart. They bring spiritual shelter that most of us need. Again, this is why the Tao Te Ching states, "When nothing is done, nothing is left undone."

In literally doing nothing, the sage is allowed to grow old and wise, bringing clarity and insight into the heart of humanity. A politician, on the other hand, is out there trying to change the world on their own watch, and, consequently, they are cut down in their prime by other people. In being plain, just like the sage, the useless tree escapes the axes of people, and so it grows vast as nature intended it.

Both the sage and the useless tree are the beneficiaries of fully embracing the nondoing nature of wu-wei. Just like the sage and the useless tree, when you return to the wu-wei nature of Tao, you will be naturally rewarded with an effortless life, free from the toil, hardship, and suffering so common within humanity.

9

Free and Easy Wandering in Oneness

The ultimate state of being for a Taoist sage, or zhenren in other words, is a freedom that can never be bound, which Chuang-tzu called *free and easy wandering*. Similar to this phrase is the Japanese *unsui*, which means to "drift like a cloud and flow like water." Unsui is the nature of an enlightened mind; it is free from all boundaries in the mind, no matter what physical circumstance one experiences. In the deepest layer beyond words, one roams freely in the spontaneous reality as it is, tzu-jan. Nothing can disturb the enlightened mind or stain it. The sage's mind doesn't retain experiences for too long, and so their mind is not bound by the past. As a result, they have no plans for the future. They are completely here and now, where consciousness always is. Most of humanity, though, lives in the fantasies of the past and future and knows nothing about the here and now.

In applying the spiritual solvent of meditation on our habit to link thoughts and also when we decrease the power our linguistic conditioning has to frame our experience, then our mind is free like a bird. Nothing, no matter what, no matter how intense, can move you once you become what you are. In the Avadhuta Gita, Lord Dattatreya explains this using a simple jar:

> When a jar is broken, the space that was inside
> Merges into the space outside.
> In the same way, my mind has merged in God;
> To me, there appears no duality.[1]

Our minds are imprisoned by the socialization process, but this book is the hammer to smash your jar. Taoism is the deprogramming technology that allows you to see again. This type of Taoist freedom is hardly known. Many in the modern world wouldn't see the value because their sole focus is on freedom from the government, having physical freedom, and so on. Taoism doesn't disagree with those sorts of freedoms, as they are part of our inalienable rights as a human being. But in the end, this is not real freedom, true Taoist freedom. If one abides in real freedom, then physical freedom won't occupy your mind. You are already free. Even though physical roaming is beneficial, especially for the Taoist, if one doesn't know true freedom, then even if you are free to move around, you'll still be enslaved by your conditioned mind. These levels of freedom are quite confusing for modern society to comprehend. The status quo is geared toward the material world, so any freedom that is nonmaterial is confusing. David Chai sums this up in regard to freedom being associated with autonomy:

> Among the many concepts that have made their way into the development of philosophical discourse, freedom is without doubt one of the more contentious. The tendency of modern society to associate it with autonomy and individualism has only contributed to the idea that freedom must be viewed as the overcoming of a challenge whose threat endangers the subject's

very existence, especially when it relates to the mind. Indeed, the contemporary world has framed the question of freedom in such a way that it has become one of the most fundamental issues of human thinking. While this may appear an insurmountable challenge, the notion that personal freedom stands in opposition to forces of restraint or constraint, be they from other people, the state, or more recently, technology, never plagued the intellectuals of ancient China—if anything, it was human desire that proved to be the major hindrance to social harmony and equality between individuals. In the case of Daoism, authentic freedom exists in only one guise—the onto-cosmological.[2]

Taoist freedom is frightening for those righteous people hellbent on social justice according to their agenda. That ignorant notion of freedom being related to autonomy and individualism is based on having goals and an aim for what is acceptable, again, according to how they subjectively see the world. That is not freedom. You are still bound to your identity and the agendas you have based on your conditioning. Real freedom has no aim, no bounds. Real freedom is aimless.

AIMLESS ROAMING

Chuang-tzu explains that real freedom is *xiaoyao you* (逍遙遊: Wade-Giles *hsiao yao yu*; Pinyin *xiaoyao you*) in Chinese. Sinologist, translator, and writer Burton Watson translated this as "free and easy wandering," while sinologist A. C. Graham translated it as "going rambling without a destination." *You* actually appears ninety-five times in the Chuang-tzu text. Obviously, *you* is very significant within the Chuang-tzu text and also for our understanding of this ultimate state of being, free and easy wandering.

You also appears with the term *xin* (心: Wade-Giles *hsin*; Pinyin *xin*), which in Chinese means "heart-mind." A. C. Graham translates *you xin* as "to let the heart-mind roam." *You xin* is applied to numerous sections in different forms with subtle, nuanced similarities in meaning. These differing forms are translated by Graham as "let the heart-mind roam in the limitless" (*you xin yu wu qiong*), "let the heart-mind roam in the flavorless" (*you xin yu dan*), and "let the heart-mind roam at the beginning of things" (*you xin yu wu zhi chu*). The mysterious nature of *you* is explained cleverly by Hans-Georg Moeller and Paul D'Ambrosio: "The sages who engage in *you*ing are not simply strolling around but seem to have entered into some extraordinary state."[3]

"Youing," as Moeller and D'Ambrosio put it, is this aimless roaming in the spontaneous reality of nature, where one has freed one's heart-mind to become a living embodiment of wu-wei. Freedom of the heart-mind allows us to embrace free and easy wandering. Philosopher Liu Xiaogan explains both terms and their relation in his article "Daoism: Laozi and Zhuangzi" in *The Oxford Handbook of World Philosophy*:

> The place in which one roams freely is mysterious as well as remote. The wilderness or the "Never-never land" (wu-he-you-zhi-xiang) refers to such a place, far beyond the world. Moreover, the compound *you xin* (mind's wandering) appears repeatedly, indicating quite directly that it is the mind, rather than the body, that roams. Thus, by combining *xiao-yao* and *you*, the *Zhuangzi* depicts a free soul roaming in the boundless world of imagination where the mysterious union with Dao can be attained. *Xiao-yao* and *you* mean gaining access to the infinite panorama of a spiritual world.[4]

The sage has completely harmonized with Tao, and its stream of consciousness moves through them unrestricted. *Xiaoyao you* is an uninhibited roaming that is aimless and directionless. One's center is everywhere and circumference nowhere. The mind is truly free; it is not entangled with world affairs and the mundane concerns of the masses. No form of conditioning diverts your awareness. Your life is no longer guided by the socialization process you've endured. You've returned home, to the way of the Tao, where freedom is your natural state of being. You wander aimlessly because nature is inherently free when you let go.

The problem is we incorrectly assume freedom is to disentangle ourselves *from* something. This is just a lower level of freedom related to our autonomy and individualism. Taoism, as you surely know by now, is to transcend individualism to merge with Tao. So real freedom is not freedom from something, but instead freedom itself. In truthfully forgetting who we were trained to be, we are free. In forgetting the artificial linguistic conventions and our qing, we are free. When we try to mold the world to suit our own self-image, we are enslaved, not free.

Governments and self-interested individuals are anxiously trying to change the world under the guise of freedom, but all that really turns out to be is tyranny and enslavement. As discussed numerous times within this book, the dissolution of the identity is essential in Taoism. It is when we forget ourselves that we begin to know true freedom. True freedom is the act of letting go and letting be, nature's way of noninterference, wu-wei. When we pursue our identity, building more layers upon it, we will likely never know or abide in our true free nature.

The sage allows life to be, so they are one with the Tao. The river of the Tao continues to flow with or without your acknowledgment. If we fight the river in trying to hold on to ourselves, then we will suffer. But if we genuinely let go and let be, then the river is our nature, because all that there is truly is the river. Fighting the current and holding on to the banks of the river are deviations from the truth, and the truth is the river continues to flow.

As one with the river, the concept of freedom disappears. Freedom itself is a concept in the linguistic framework to discern a state beyond being bound. But when you are one with the river, then you are naturally what freedom is pointing to. We forget the concept of freedom and aimlessly roam without any borders within or without. This, as I've said, is not individual freedom, but rather an awakening to the Tao in all life; as David Chai states:

> The assumption that freedom only pertains to the human guise of being, rather than all beings, would appear irrational to Zhuangzi. If we are to speak of freedom being tied to Dao, we cannot refer to it in language of the free and not-free, for Dao is neither. To be free thus involves letting-go of freedom such that the concept of freedom vanishes completely. For Zhuangzi, freedom in Dao is hence the cosmological harmonization of things through which one partakes in a carefree wandering that is neither hindered nor tainted by concerns over what it means to be free. There is, therefore, no such thing as individual freedom; rather, freedom presents itself as a great awakening to the nothingness incipient in all things.[5]

From the lofty vantage point of Tao, all things are free. This is the fundamental truth. Everything is nondual in oneness; there is actually no separation. As discussed, this true freedom is beyond the concept of freedom. A sage's real freedom is not becoming free from barriers placed upon them but rather a reflection of their heart-mind grounded in the original nothingness of Tao. They are a reflection of that nothingness and so the concept of a border or boundary has no meaning. Hence, freedom from "something" is an illusion bound to those who suffer from the border of their identity.

Real freedom is in the nothingness of Tao, our original face before the socialization process warped our nature. Our return motion is to become harmonious with the Tao, a reflection of nothingness. Through the power of wu-wei and aimless roaming, we harmonize with the world. We become perfectly calibrated to life. The harmony of freedom is explained in the Chuang-tzu text with *the three heavenly principles* of measurement, differentiation, and harmony:

> *What is called harmonizing things with heavenly differentiation? It is said that affirming and not affirming are the same, as are the so and not-so. If the so is really so, then as it is clearly different from the not-so, there is no need to differentiate them. If affirmation is really affirming, then as it is clearly different from not affirming, there is no need to differentiate them. The transformation of [wind] into sound is a mutual dependency that is, at the same time, not mutually dependent. Harmonize them with heavenly differentiation, allow them to mutually clarify each other, and in this way, you can complete your allotted years. Forget about years and standards, stop and only take the infinite as your end, and in the infinite, you shall dwell.[6]*

Harmonizing in this Taoist freedom is a byproduct of letting go of oneself and consequently letting the world be without any interference. Your being, then, is not bound. But we are clinging to ourselves like a child clinging to a kite without letting it fly. Once we fly, our projection associated to identity vanishes, and this allows us to be as the Tao *is*. Just as the Tao loves and nourishes all but does not lord it over them, so do we. In harmonizing with the Tao, our love is unassociated. Being grounded in oneness gives us an awareness of the whole.

The Tao does not favor anyone. We all live, die, and return to the source. Cognitive errors such as anthropocentrism dissolve from letting life be. Everything is a vast spiritual panorama of Tao, so how could we favor anything? All is Tao and Tao is all. Harmonizing with the way of nature is the heavenly course of the universe, and the heavenly is Tao.

The unassociated love intrinsic to the Tao becomes our modus operandi. We have the warmth and tender care of a grandmother and also the wisdom and humility of an old sage. Favoritism is gone, and life will be as life will be. A sage is a piece of life, not a separate entity from it. To become a piece of life, as one with it, we must dissolve the identity or ego. Then and only then will you experience real Taoist freedom. But to dissolve the identity and discover this lofty freedom, we must let go and let be. We must emulate the great sages.

LAO-TZU AND CHUANG-TZU'S ART OF LIBERATION

The common person knows secular freedom but not Taoist freedom. Secular freedom is dependent on external circumstances matching one's own beliefs and identity. The average person, then, is possessed by control. When we lose control of the way we want life to be, we essentially lose ourselves in the worst possible way. Anger, anxiety, and abuse spawn from our version of reality being humbled by life. Taoism is that very technology to destroy your identity and consequently your urge to control, while allowing the possibility of trust to flower.

Most of us want certainty. We at least want to know the direction we are going. The sage, on the other hand, aimlessly wanders in the emptiness of the Tao. To master uninhibited roaming, one must trust. Trust is the result of wu-wei, letting go and letting be. The sage is completely liberated and could never be brought back down into the world of illusion.

Sincere trust evokes joy. On the other hand, the average person's lack of trust and urge for control are the result of politically oriented people, and politics are divisive in their disposition. The political person lives in fear and is aggressive, even though they've conned themselves into believing they are righteous and arbiters of freedom (of course, according to their own personal view). They are those overly serious people who are exhausting to be around, taking their own opinion as gospel and essentially thinking too highly of themselves. They are prisoners in their own mind and cannot walk free. Contrary to this imprisoned political nature is the sage, walking free without a care in the world. The sage has no axe to grind, no teaching or worldview to spread. They have no mission.

Wandering in the infinite reality of Tao is a joy the divisive political person (or most people in general) is not ready for. Instead of seriousness, the sage is playful and has restored their child-like innocence. This results from the sage's individual will down-regulating to allow the Tao to move through them. Their natural instincts are harmonious with life, as this carefree spontaneity is our inborn nature. Aimless wandering is the living constitution of oneness, while control and certainty are unnatural and in conflict with oneness.

The average person is so dedicated to being somebody, validated by titles, status, and respect from others. The sage is bemused by such insecurity and trusts the universe, and so aimless roaming in the Tao is their way of life. As a result, the sage lives life with a playful ignorance and is not concerned by status, titles, wealth, or adulation from others. The sage is firmly grounded in the Tao, and they live in pure joy because their mind is equanimous. The sage has no reason for being playful or joyful; they are naturally in those states for the sake of them. Just like love, our playfulness and joy are usually associated with something, but the sage lives in the empty unassociated world of Tao, where nature is spontaneously of itself (tzu-jan). The wandering of the sage, then, is not just to pass the time, but rather a living expression of the Tao in its empty, spontaneous nature.

Free and easy wandering is the effortless flow of consciousness into the infinite possibilities presented by the Tao of nothingness once we make our return. The sage lives in the timeless and wanders where no one has gone before. This is Lao-tzu and Chuang-tzu's art of liberation. Nothing within them remains, eclipsing their true oneness with Tao. Lao-tzu and Chuang-tzu were dedicated to the uncarved block while Confucius went in a different direction, the same direction we all mistakenly take, the carving and polishing way of life.

Confucius could never master the art of liberation because his worldview was upside down due to his belief that we are beasts from birth who need to be cultivated. All of Confucius's ideals, as a result, belong to the human socialized world and have literally nothing to do with the mystical reality of Tao, even though he may have thought so. If Confucius could have inquired into his own nature and uprooted his own agenda, then he could have walked carefree in the Tao with the great masters. He forgot his original face, and so he severed himself from the Tao more and more. Confucius even admits that if someone masters their socialized virtues, they are still worlds away from being one with the Tao:

They are men who wander beyond boundaries; I, however, am one who wanders within boundaries. . . . They see man's body as being the composition of different substances coming together in one form. They forget their liver and gall, their ears and eyes; over and over they end and they begin, not knowing head from tail. Peaceful and carefree they occupy themselves in what lies beyond the dust and dirt of the world, roaming carefree in the spirit of non-deliberate doing. How can they irritate themselves with such practiced etiquette so as to impress the views of common people's ears and eyes![7]

Confucius knows his process of cultural indoctrination cannot infect one who is aimlessly roaming in wu-wei, as he admitted. He never knew free and easy wandering because, like most people, he still had an axe to grind. When we are so engaged with the world, like Confucius was, we can never abide in the Tao and be at true ease. This was his plight, but it must not be yours.

By sincerely practicing wu-wei and not engaging in the world, the sage wanders the world untouched by debates of this and that. Their heart-mind is completely free. Free and easy wandering harmonizes us with the Tao. With no concern, no agenda, and no identity, we are free. Aimlessly wandering in the nothingness of Tao means we've transcended the dualistic hypnosis of humanity and instead walk free in the real oneness of Tao.

The sage experiences reality in its wholeness, as nature is and intended for us, that is until socialization stepped in. Their identity has been cleansed out so that they don't experience reality in a fragmented way. They are literally the eyes and ears of the Tao, as they see with spirit and not mind, to paraphrase Chuang-tzu's words. The beingness of the sage has been set free from the artificial cage we accumulate throughout life. The sage is the genuine essence of the universe, zhenren, and their nature is freedom itself. Once we embody this real freedom, then we, too, can roam carefree in the eternal plenitude of Tao.

RETURNING HOME

Tao sets us free; the world holds us hostage. Our choice is an easy one, but the energy and power the world has over us is immense. However, to be like Lao-tzu and Chuang-tzu, we need to ride like the wind and learn to have variation through the rising tides of change. No matter what the universe throws at you, you will move as Cook Ting in harmony with the whole. As a result, you live with the ease that Chuang-tzu alluded to.

A million problems could surface, and you are untouched by any of them. You are not blown here or there by the world. Your heart is not moved by what the world values or believes is important. You embody this ease because your mind is a mirror of the meontological nature of Tao. Your mind is a reflection of space because space is empty, and yet it contains the entire universe.

When nothing can leave an impression in your mind, you are free. People will be confused at first at your ease, just as the common folk were confused by the ease of Lao-tzu and Chuang-tzu. But your presence will be felt, not by force but instead by a silence and ease that reverberates throughout the universe. This is the grace of Tao. This same grace is why twenty-five hundred years later we are still reading and positively being influenced by the eternal truth of the Tao Te Ching and Chuang-tzu texts.

Your awakening is the great boon the universe is waiting for. Nothing intrinsically makes us lesser than Lao-tzu and Chuang-tzu. The only difference is the illusion of self you hold on to. You've been grasping it for so long. Aren't you tired? It is time to let go and let Tao.

To let Tao opens our consciousness completely. The disintegration of identity leads to an expansion of consciousness where it has no boundaries and is completely free. This occurs because, in truth, consciousness is everywhere and not local. Consciousness does not only reside in the brain, as many scientists and physicalists suggest. We are just like the jar analogy from the Avadhuta Gita; our consciousness is trapped in the identity of the jar and yearns to merge with the one consciousness outside identity (jar). Our localization of the one consciousness identifies with the equipment on the local level (body-mind matrix), and we continue to suffer because we are imprisoned within our ego, identity, and self. But even though we do our best to hold on to this illusion, at the death of our mortal body, we are forced to let go.

At death our body and mind disintegrate back into Tao or Brahman. The quest of the spiritual aspirant is to not wait until death for this disintegration to occur. We can achieve this while living, and this is the individual liberation of the *Jivanmukta*, a Sanskrit word or title denoting one who is liberated in this life. They have attained enlightenment and walk free in the nothingness of Tao. The sage or Jivanmukta disintegrates their ego and returns home while living to be one with Tao.

In our completion of our return home, we learn how to truly live and remain in the comforting current of the river of Tao. We flow as one with the river, traversing the breadth and length with a carefree joy. As a result, we regain our natural state of traversing the universe (river of Tao) not by our confused identity, but rather by our prajna intuition. This natural intuition belongs to the oneness of Tao. You will act and react immediately and appropriately to every situation with patience and love. You are no longer possessing life nor are you possessed by the so-called separate components of life because your prajna intuition is the result of a consciousness firmly rooted in oneness. No separation exists as all is whole.

Wandering aimlessly in Tao allows your prajna intuition to function naturally, where unassociated love is your foundation. Only love can exist when you're home in the oneness of Tao. If there truly is no other, then love is all that there is. Fear is the result of a belief in separation that makes individuals feel isolated. But the one who is isolated, the conditioned identity, is the child of a world built on fear. So your identity is the result of fear, not love. As discussed throughout this book, we utterly need to let that identity go so that we can allow our true nature, love, to shine and bring spiritual oxygen into a world on life support.

You will walk effortlessly among them, but the concept of "them" has disappeared. You allow them to be as they will, as you continue your free and easy wandering in the eternal beauty of Tao. Your love will extend to all because all is Tao. All conflict and confusion in the world are due to a lack of understanding that all is Tao, so our love and consequently our hate are built on the concept of separation. But separation never existed, it was only a dream, and much bloodshed has been spilled from this hypnotic illusion, turning the dream into a nightmare.

There was and can only ever be the Tao. When we genuinely know this, then the love that we truly are will be the love we share with all. In our return, we will live in peace and harmony on this Earth because there is only the oneness state of consciousness that is Tao. This is not a utopian vision, but rather the actuality of the oneness of consciousness, the nature of Tao we embody once we return home. The Tao greets us with a loving embrace as we return from our long journey into the illusion of duality. We feel its warmth, the unconditional love of oneness we once thought was a myth. If the Tao could speak, it would say, "You've been gone for so long. I've missed you, my dear one. Welcome home."

Notes

INTRODUCTION. RECLAIMING TAOISM

1. Capra, *Tao of Physics*, 124.

1. THE HUMAN REFLECTION OF THE UNIVERSE

1. Lao Tsu, *Tao Te Ching*, trans. Feng and English, xvi.
2. Lao Tsu, *Tao Te Ching*, trans. Feng and English, 7.
3. Chuang Tsu, *Chuang Tsu*, 29.
4. Lao Tsu, *Tao Te Ching*, trans. Feng and English, 45.
5. Jiddu Krishnamurti, "J. Krishnamurti - Brockwood Park 1983— Conversation 1 with D. Bohm—Is there an action not touched by thought?," J. Krishnamurti's official channel, streamed Jan. 7, 2014, YouTube video, 1:20:17.
6. Lao Tsu, *Tao Te Ching*, trans. Feng and English, 18.
7. Lao Tzu, *Hua Hu Ching*, 103.
8. Lao Tsu, *Tao Te Ching*, trans. Feng and English, 27.
9. Lao Tsu, *Tao Te Ching*, trans. Feng and English, 39.
10. Lao Tsu, *Tao Te Ching*, trans. Feng and English, xxi.
11. Watts, *Tao: The Watercourse Way*, 15.

2. TAOISM'S CRITIQUE OF CONFUCIANISM AND SOCIALIZATION

1. Quoted in Moeller and D'Ambrosio, *Genuine Pretending*, 9.
2. Quote from a letter to Bishop Mandell Creighton, April 5, 1887, published in J. N. Figgis and R. V. Laurence, eds., *Historical Essays and Studies* (Macmillan, 1907).
3. Moeller and D'Ambrosio, *Genuine Pretending*, 8.
4. Moeller, *Philosophy of the Daodejing*, 108.
5. Chuang Tzu, *Complete Works*, 327.
6. Chuang Tzu, *Complete Works*, 326.
7. Moeller and D'Ambrosio, *Genuine Pretending*, 110.

3. THE DISSOLUTION OF IDENTITY

1. Chuang Tzu, *Complete Works*, 97.
2. Laozi, *Daodejing*, trans. Moeller, 123.
3. Huxley, *Perennial Philosophy*, 77.
4. Huxley, *Perennial Philosophy*, 77.
5. "Fight Club (Film)," Wikiquote website, last modified December 23, 2024, 14:05.
6. Chuang Tzu, *Complete Works*, 57–58.

4. THE IMMORALITY OF MORALITY

1. Lao Tsu, *Tao Te Ching*, trans. Feng and English, 21.
2. Lao Tsu, *Tao Te Ching*, trans. Feng and English, 20.
3. Deepak, *India that is Bharat*.
4. Malhotra, *Being Different*, 16.
5. Malhotra, *Being Different*, 21.
6. Malhotra, *Being Different*, 19.
7. Malhotra, *Being Different*, 26.
8. Damo Mitchell, "It is possible to form your view of the world and society from your direct experience rather than the view that is given to you by media and government," Instagram website, August 15, 2021.

9. Watts, *Way of Zen*, 26.

10. "Wikipedia: Ox Mountain," Wikimedia Foundation, last updated October 30, 2023.

5. BEYOND GOOD AND EVIL

1. Pattanaik, *7 Secrets of Shiva*, 197.
2. Pattanaik, *7 Secrets of Shiva*, 45.
3. Chuang Tsu, *Chuang Tsu*, 29.
4. Center for International Development, "Panel: The Moral Sentiment of Us," Center for International Development channel, Global Empowerment Meeting, streamed May 9, 2018, YouTube video, 28:30.
5. Krishnamurti, *Krishnamurti*, 94.
6. Lao Tzu, *Tao Te Ching*, trans. Lin, 11.
7. Baynes, *I Ching or Book of Changes*, 78.

6. THE SIMPLE WORLD VS. THE COMPLEX WORLD

1. Chai, *Zhuangzi and the Becoming of Nothingness*, 28.
2. Laozi, *Daodejing of Laozi*, trans. Ivanhoe, 12.
3. Lao Tzu, *Tao Te Ching*, trans Lau, 69.
4. Laozi, *Daodejing of Laozi*, trans. Ivanhoe, 37.
5. Laozi, *Daodejing of Laozi*, trans. Ivanhoe, 50.
6. Chuang Tzu, *Complete Works*, 50–51.

7. THE ART OF DOING NOTHING

1. Radhakrishnan, *Bhagavadgita*, 136.
2. Chai, *Zhuangzi and the Becoming of Nothingness*, 35.
3. Chai, *Zhuangzi and the Becoming of Nothingness*, 83.
4. Chai, *Zhuangzi and the Becoming of Nothingness*, 116.
5. Chai, *Zhuangzi and the Becoming of Nothingness*, 121.
6. Maharshi, *Be As You Are*, 26.

8. THE
SPONTANEOUS REALITY

1. Suzuki, *Essays in East-West Philosophy*, 18, 24, 41.
2. Blofeld, *Zen Teaching of Hui Hai*, 56.
3. Blofeld, *Zen Teaching of Huang Po*, 54.
4. Chuang Tzu, *Complete Works*, 65.

9. FREE AND EASY
WANDERING IN ONENESS

1. Dattatreya, *Dattatreya's Song of the Avadhut*, 27.
2. Chai, *Zhuangzi and the Becoming of Nothingness*, 139.
3. Moeller and D'Ambrosio, *Genuine Pretending*, 165.
4. Liu Xiaogan, "Daoism: Laozi and Zhuangzi," in Garfield and Edelglass, *Oxford Handbook of World Philosophy*, 54.
5. Chai, *Zhuangzi and the Becoming of Nothingness*, 143,
6. Chai, *Zhuangzi and the Becoming of Nothingness*, 144–45.
7. Chai, *Zhuangzi and the Becoming of Nothingness*, 163.

Bibliography

Austin, James. *Zen and the Brain: Toward an Understanding of Meditation and Consciousness.* Cambridge, Mass.: MIT Press, 1999.

Baynes, Cary F., trans. *The I Ching or Book of Changes: The Richard Wilhelm Translation rendered into English by Cary F. Baynes.* Princeton, N.J.: Princeton University Press, 1967.

Benoit, Hubert. *Zen and the Psychology of Transformation: The Supreme Doctrine.* Rochester, Vt.: Inner Traditions, 1990.

Blofeld, John. *Taoism: Road to Immortality.* Boston, Mass.: Shambhala, 2000.

Blofeld, John, trans. *The Zen Teaching of Huang Po: On the Transmission of Mind.* New York: Grove Press, 1994.

Blofeld, John, trans. *The Zen Teaching of Hui Hai: On Sudden Illumination.* London: Rider & Company, 1969.

Bodhi, Bhikkhu. *In the Buddha's Words: An Anthology of the Discourses from the Pali Canon.* Somerville, Mass.: Wisdom Publications, 2005.

Bodhidharma. *The Zen Teachings of Bodhidharma.* Translated by Red Pine. Berkeley, Calif.: North Point Press, 1989.

Campbell, Joseph. *Myths of Light: Eastern Metaphors of the Eternal.* Novato, Calif.: New World Library, 2003.

Campbell, Joseph. *Pathways to Bliss: Mythology and Personal Transformation.* Novato, Calif.: New World Library, 2004.

Campbell, Joseph. *The Power of Myth.* New York: Anchor Books, 1991.

Capra, Fritjof. *The Tao of Physics: An Exploration of the Parallels between Modern Physics and Eastern Mysticism.* Boston, Mass.: Shambhala, 2000.

Chai, David. *Zhuangzi and the Becoming of Nothingness.* New York: Suny Press, 2019.

Chuang Tsu. *Chuang Tsu: Inner Chapters, a Companion to Tao Te Ching.* Translated by Gia-Fu Feng and Jane English. Portland, Ore.: Amber Lotus, 2008.

Chuang Tzu. *The Complete Works of Chuang Tzu.* Translated by Burton Watson. New York: Columbia University Press, 1968.

Clark, Andy. *Being There: Putting Brain, Body, and World Together Again.* Cambridge, Mass.: A Bradford Book, 1997.

Cleary, Thomas, trans. *The Taoism Reader.* Boston, Mass.: Shambhala, 2012.

Confucius. *Analects: With Selections from Traditional Commentaries.* Translated by Edward Slingerland. Indianapolis, Ind.: Hackett Publishing, 2003.

Csikszentmihalyi, Mihaly. *Flow: The Psychology of Optimal Experience.* New York: Harper & Row, 1990.

Dattatreya. *Dattatreya's Song of the Avadhut: An English Translation of the Avadhut Gita.* Translated by Swami Abhayananda. Delhi, India: Atma Books, 2000.

Deepak, J. Sai. *India that is Bharat: Coloniality, Civilisation, Constitution.* New Delhi, India: Bloomsbury India, 2021.

Dennett, Daniel. *Consciousness Explained.* Boston, Mass.: Back Bay Books, 1991.

Dietrich, Arne. *Introduction to Consciousness.* London: Palgrave Macmillan, 2007.

Durkheim, Emile. *The Elementary Forms of Religious Life.* New York: Oxford, 2008.

Dyer, Wayne W. *Wisdom of the Ages: 60 Days to Enlightenment.* New York: William Morrow, 2002.

Easwaran, Eknath, trans. *The Upanishads.* Tomales, Calif.: Nilgiri Press, 2007.

Flanagan, Owen. *The Bodhisattva's Brain: Buddhism Naturalized.* Cambridge, Mass.: A Bradford Book, 2013.

Garfield, Jay L., and William Edelglass. *The Oxford Handbook of World Philosophy.* New York: Oxford University Press, 2011.

Gaudapada and Sankara. *The Mandukya Upanishad.* Translated by Swami Nikhilananda. Kolkata, India: Advaita Ashrama, 2019.

Gregory, Jason. *Effortless Living.* Rochester, Vt.: Inner Traditions, 2018.

Gregory, Jason. *Emotional Intuition for Peak Performance.* Rochester, Vt.: Inner Traditions, 2020.

Gregory, Jason. *Enlightenment Now*. Rochester, Vt.: Inner Traditions, 2016.

Gregory, Jason. *Fasting the Mind*. Rochester, Vt.: Inner Traditions, 2017.

Gregory, Jason. *The Science and Practice of Humility*. Rochester, Vt.: Inner Traditions, 2014.

Gregory, Jason. *Spiritual Freedom in the Digital Age*. Hampshire, UK: O-Books, 2022.

Griffith, Ralph T. H. *The Hymns of the Rgveda*. Delhi, India: Motilal Banarsidass Publishers, 1999.

Guenon, Rene. *The Essential Rene Guenon*. Bloomington, Ind.: World Wisdom, 2009.

Hanh, Thich Nhat. *Silence: The Power of Quiet in a World Full of Noise*. London: Rider, 2015.

Hanson, Rick. *Buddha's Brain: The Practical Neuroscience of Happiness, Love, and Wisdom*. Oakland, Calif.: New Harbinger Publications, 2009.

Hart, William. *The Art of Living: Vipassana Meditation*. New York: Harper One, 1987.

Holman, John. *The Return of the Perennial Philosophy*. London: Watkins, 2008.

Huang Po. *The Zen Teaching of Huang Po*. Translated by John Blofeld. New York: Grove Press, 1994.

Hui Hai. *The Zen Teaching of Hui Hai*. Translated by John Blofeld. London: Rider, 1969.

Huxley, Aldous. *The Perennial Philosophy*. New York: Harper Perennial Modern Classics, 2009.

Ivanhoe, Philip J., and Bryan W. Van Norden. *Readings in Classical Chinese Philosophy*. Indianapolis, Ind.: Hackett Publishing Company, 2005.

Kahneman, Daniel, *Thinking, Fast and Slow*. London: Penguin, 2012.

Kelly, Brendan. *The Yin and Yang of Climate Crisis: Healing Personal, Cultural, and Ecological Imbalance with Chinese Medicine*. Berkeley, Calif.: North Atlantic Books, 2015.

Kingsley, Peter. *Reality*. Point Reyes, Calif.: The Golden Sufi Center, 2004.

Krishnamurti, Jiddu. *Krishnamurti on Education*. Chennai, India: Krishnamurti Foundation India, 2012.

Krishnamurti, Jiddu. *Krishnamurti: Reflections on the Self*. Chicago: Open Court, 1998.

Krishnamurti, Jiddu. *Total Freedom: The Essential Krishnamurti*. New York: Harper One, 1996.

Lao Tsu. *Tao Te Ching*. Translated by Gia-Fu Feng and Jane English. New York: Vintage Books, 2011.

Lao Tzu. *Hua Hu Ching*. Translated by Hua-Ching Ni. Boston, Mass.: Shambhala, 1995.

Lao Tzu. *Tao Te Ching*. Translated by D. C. Lau. Hong Kong: The Chinese University Press, 1989.

Lao Tzu. *Tao Te Ching*. Translated by Derek Lin. Woodstock, Vt.: SkyLight Paths, 2006.

Lao Tzu. *Tao Te Ching: An Illustrated Journey*. Translated by Stephen Mitchell. London: Frances Lincoln, 2009.

Laozi. *Daodejing: The New, Highly Readable Translation of the Life-Changing Ancient Scripture Formerly Known as the Tao Te Ching*. Translated by Hans-Georg Moeller. Chicago: Open Court, 2007.

Laozi. *The Daodejing of Laozi*. Translated by Philip J. Ivanhoe. Indianapolis, Ind.: Hackett Publishing Company, 2003.

Liu I-Ming. *Awakening to the Tao*. Translated by Thomas Cleary. Boston, Mass.: Shambhala, 1988.

Loy, David R. *Nonduality in Buddhism and Beyond*. Somerville, Mass.: Wisdom Publications, 2019.

Maharshi, Sri Ramana. *Be As You Are: The Teaching of Sri Ramana Maharshi*. Translated by David Godman. Delhi, India: Penguin Books, 1992.

Maharshi, Sri Ramana. *Saddarsanam and An Inquiry into the Revelation of Truth and Oneself*. Translated by Nome. Santa Cruz, Calif: Society of Abidance in Truth, 2009.

Malhotra, Rajiv. *Being Different: An Indian Challenge to Western Universalism*. India: Harper Collins Publishers India, 2011.

Masters, Robert Augustus. *Spiritual Bypassing: When Spirituality Disconnects us from What Really Matters*. Berkeley, Calif.: North Atlantic Books, 2010.

Mengzi. *Mengzi: With Sections from Traditional Commentaries*. Translated by Bryan W. Van Norden. Indianapolis, Ind.: Hackett Publishing, 2008.

Merton, Thomas. *The Way of Chuang Tzu*. New York: New Directions, 2010.

Ming-Dao, Deng. *Everyday Tao: Living with Balance and Harmony*. New York: Harper Collins, 1996.

Ming-Dao, Deng. *The Living I Ching: Using Ancient Chinese Wisdom to Shape Your Life*. New York: Harper Collins, 2006.

Mitchell, Damo. *A Comprehensive Guide to Nei Gong*. London: Singing Dragon, 2018.

Moeller, Hans-Georg. *The Philosophy of the Daodejing*. New York: Columbia University Press, 2006.

Moeller, Hans-Georg, and Paul J. D'Ambrosio. *Genuine Pretending: On the Philosophy of the Zhuangzi*. New York: Columbia University Press, 2017.

Nikhilananda, Swami. *The Bhagavad Gita*. New Delhi, India: Fingerprint! Classics, 2023.

Nikhilananda, Swami. *Self-Knowledge (Atmabodha): An English Translation of Sankaracharya's Atmabodha with Notes, Comments, and Introduction*. New York: Ramakrishna-Vedanta Center, 1974.

Nisbett, Richard E. *The Geography of Thought*. New York: Free Press, 2003.

Olivelle, Patrick, trans. *Upaniṣads*. New York: Oxford University Press, 1996.

Ouspensky, P. D. *In Search of the Miraculous: The Teachings of G. I. Gurdjieff*. Orlando, Fla.: Harvest Book Harcourt, 2001.

Patanjali. *The Yoga-Sutra of Patanjali: A New Translation with Commentary*. Translated and commentary by Chip Hartranft. Boston, Mass.: Shambhala, 2003.

Pattanaik, Devdutt. *7 Secrets of Shiva*. Chennai, India: Westland, 2011.

Pine, Red. *The Heart Sutra*. Berkeley, Calif.: Counterpoint, 2005.

Pinker, Steven. *How the Mind Works*. New York: W. W. Norton and Company, 1997.

Pinker, Steven. *The Language Instinct: How the Mind Creates Language*. New York: Harper Perennial Modern Classics, 2007.

Radhakrishnan, Sarvepalli. *The Bhagavadgita: with an Introductory Essay, Sanskrit Text, English Translation and Notes*. Noida, India: Harper Collins India, 2010.

Reid, Daniel. *The Tao of Health, Sex, and Longevity*. New York: Simon and Schuster, 1989.

Schuon, Frithjof. *The Transcendent Unity of Religions*. Wheaton, Ill.: Quest Books, 1984.

Shankara. *Shankara's Crest Jewel of Discrimination*. Translated by Swami Prabhavananda and Christopher Isherwood. Los Angeles: Vedanta Society of Southern California, 1975.

Slingerland, Edward, and Mark Collard, eds. *Creating Consilience: Integrating the Sciences and the Humanities*. New York: Oxford, 2012.

Slingerland, Edward. *Trying Not to Try: The Art and Science of Spontaneity.* New York: Crown, 2014.

Suzuki, Daisetsu Teitaro. *Essays in East-West Philosophy: An Attempt at World Philosophical Synthesis.* Edited by Charles Alexander Moore. Honolulu: University of Hawaii Press, 2021.

Suzuki, Daisetsu Teitaro, trans. *The Lankavatara Sutra: A Mahayana Text.* Philadelphia, Pa.: Coronet Books, 1999.

Suzuki, Shunryu. *Zen Mind, Beginner's Mind: Informal Talks on Zen Meditation and Practice.* Boston, Mass.: Shambhala, 2011.

Watts, Alan. *Become What You Are.* Boston, Mass.: Shambhala, 2003.

Watts, Alan. *The Book: On the Taboo Against Knowing Who You Are.* New York: Vintage Books, 1989.

Watts, Alan. *Do You Do It, or Does It Do You?: How to Let the Universe Meditate You.* Narrated by the author. Louisville, Colo.: Sounds True Audio, 2005. 4 hr., 15 min.

Watts, Alan. *Out of Your Mind: Essential Listening from the Alan Watts Audio Archives.* Narrated by the author. Louisville, Colo.: Sounds True Audio, 2004. 14 hr., 15 min.

Watts, Alan. *Tao: The Watercourse Way.* New York: Pantheon, 1977.

Watts, Alan. *The Way of Zen.* New York: Vintage Books, 1999.

Watts, Alan. *The Wisdom of Insecurity: A Message for an Age of Anxiety.* New York: Vintage Books, 2011.

Welwood, John. *Toward a Psychology of Awakening: Buddhism, Psychotherapy, and the Path of Personal and Spiritual Transformation.* Boston, Mass.: Shambhala, 2002.

Wilhelm, Richard. *The Secret of the Golden Flower: A Chinese Book of Life.* London: Arkana, 1984.

Wong, Eva. *Cultivating Stillness: A Taoist Manual for Transforming Body and Mind.* Boston, Mass.: Shambhala, 1992.

Xunzi. *Xunzi: Basic Writings.* Translated by Burton Watson. New York: Columbia University Press, 2003.

Index

Abrahamic religions, and sin, 91–93
accent (spoken), 120
accepting ourselves, 12–13
action
   and its fruits, 150
   resisting the urge to act, 152
Advaita Vedanta, 116–17, 160, 162–63
advertising, 137–38
"All is Brahman," 163
American dream, the, 139
"An eye for an eye . . .," 126
anthropocentric illusion, the, 72–77
anxiety, 142
Arjuna, 30, 149–50, 152
ash, 114–15
ashrams, 151–53
Atman, 162–63, 176
   and Brahman, 30
Avadhuta Gita, 181, 192
awe, 175

bellows metaphor, 18–19, 83
belonging, 76
Benedict, Pope, 96
Bhagavad Gita, 30, 149–50

big bang, 27
big picture, and small picture, 16
body, as covering, 116–17
Brahma, 24
Brahman, 65, 80, 162–63, 192
   and Atman, 30
   as only reality, 160
Brahmanda, 130
   defined, 112–13
Buddha, 169
Buddha-mind, 171
busyness, 69
   and the illusion of identity,
     150–54

Capra, Fritjof, 4
carving and polishing metaphor,
   44–45
certainty, desire for, 187–88
Chai, David, 133, 181–82
   on freedom, 185
chase and the hunt, the, 41, 148
chengwang, defined, 160
child-and-well metaphor, 106–8
Chinese words, romanization of, xii

Christianity
  and anthropocentrism, 72–74
  Christians condemning Nepalis, 90
  morality of, 89–90, 118
  and sexual orientation, 92–93
Chuang-tzu, 80–84, 142–46, 154, 160, 177–78. *See also* Taoism; Taoist sage
  biographical information, 8
  dates of, 3
  on death, 11
  his art of liberation, 189
  his wish to work with nature, 73
  humor of, 55–60
  Hundun story of, 66–79
  on qing, 110–11
  as root sage of Taoism, 7–9
  on wu chi, 19
Chuang-tzu text, incorrect translations of, 1–2
closing the entries, 67–68
complex world, vs simple world, 132–48
conciousness, as nonlocal, 191–92
conflict, caused by separation, 124
conformity, Hundun and, 69–70
Confucianism, 43–62
  artificiality of, 50
  and the art of liberation, 189–90
  Confucian morality, 47–55
  as prevailing school in China, 44
  roles in, 49
  rules in, 103–8
  stress and, 50–51
  Taoism's critique of, 26, 43–62, 86, 103–8
  vanity and, 52–55
  worthlessness and, 51–52

Confucius, 44–45, 49, 103–5, 189–90
  and fasting the mind, 81–84
  and Robber Chih, 55–60
construction, 112
consumerism, 139, 171
consumption of resources, 75
contentment, of contentment, 142
control, 33–34
Cook Ting, 142–47, 191
Copernicus, Nicolaus, 79
cosmology of the Tao, 16–22, 66
creativity, 129–30
cultural appropriation, 5–7
culture, as not your friend, 78

Dalberg-Acton, John, 52
D'Ambrosio, Paul J., 48, 52–53, 61, 183
Dark Side of the Moon, The, 132
Dattatreya, Lord, 181
Dayananda Saraswati, Swami, 95–96
death, 11, 171–72, 192
Deepak, J. Sai, 89
demographic swamping, 89
deprogramming, Taoism as, 4, 12, 181
Descartes, Rene, 153
desires of the belly, 136–37, 140–42
desires of the eye, 136–39
dharma, defined, 150
differences, and similarities, 124
differentiation, 186
doctrinal privilege, the end of, 93–97
dogs, and socialization, 133–34
doing nothing. *See also* wu-wei
  the art of, 149–64
drishti, defined, 132
duality, 101–2
Dzogchen, 172

Earth, 21, 28
Eastern culture, and relaxation of
    rules, 102–3
Eastern spirituality, 125, 153
    as not expansionist, 90
education, and socialization, 134–35
effortless action, 9–10, 34, 149–50.
    See also wu-wei
ego-death, 172
ego identity, 22–23
    dissolution of, 63–84
    removing the, 30
emotions, 129
emptiness, 129
    and fasting the mind, 82–83
enlightenment, described, 64–65
evil, beyond good and, 109–31

fake sincerity, 48–50
family, as root of social order, 57
fasting the mind, 67, 80–83, 127,
    164, 168
Fibonacci, Leonardo, 37
Fight Club, 77–78
filling the openings, 68
Five Elements, Chinese, 17–18
    illustration, 17
footprint story, 154–55
forgetting that which is real, 160
forget yourself, 158–62, 159–60
    vs. forgetting that which is real, 160
four pillars of separation, 118–22,
    176–77
free and easy wandering, 159,
    180–93
    defined, 182–83
    as joy, 188–90
    and prajna intuition, 192–93
    and Taoism, 5–6

freedom, 180–82
    concept disappears, 185
    is not disentangling, 184
    and liberation, 187–90
    and unlearning, 63
freedom of speech, 99
fundamental forces, 14–15

Gandhi, Mahatma, 97, 126
genuine person, 158–59. *See also*
    Taoist sage
    defined, 60–61
good and evil, beyond, 109–31
goodness, 106–8
Graham, A. C., 182
great undoing, the, 142–47
Gregory, Jason (author), his
    knowledge of Taoism, ix–x
guilt, 102
guru-disciple relationship, 41

Haidt, Jonathan, 120
Hanh, Thich Nhat, 150–51
harmony, 22, 103, 186
    harmonizing, 186–87
    natural, 35–42, 57
heart-mind, 159
Heaven, 21, 28
Heidegger, Martin, 138–39
hesitation, 169
Hinduism
    as safe haven for cultures, 88–89
    three divine principles in, 24
holism, and Taoism, 3
home, returning, 191–93
Hu, 67, 69–71, 73
Hua Hu Ching, 28
Huai-nan-tzu, 66
Huang Po, 173

Hui Hai, 170–71
human becoming, 141
human being, 141
  as model of the whole, 27–31
  as not special, 75–76
humanity, embracing via Taoism,
  11–12
humility, 25–27, 177
  and the sage, 147–48
humor, in Taoism, 56
Hundred Schools of Thought, 43
Hundun, 66–79
  as center of the world, 72
  and conformity, 69–70
  death of, 67–68, 70–72
  defined, 66
  failure of, 70–72
  in Hundun's image, 77–79
  as wholeness, 66
Hun-tun, 67
Huxley, Aldous, 73–74, 97

"I," 153
  and conflict, 124–25
  death of ego, 172
  thinking and the illusion of self,
    166–69
I Ching, 130–31
identity
  being nobody, 153–54
  and busyness, 150–54
  dissolution of, 63–84, 79, 184,
    192–93
  fear of dissolution of, 64–65
  as illusion, 123, 150, 155
  as insecure and limited, 123–27
illusion, 112
impartiality, 128–31, 131
India, radical acceptance in, 126

indifference to the world, 8
individualism, 74
Inevitable Progress, 73, 75
inferiority complex, 51
interference, Taoism as a critique
  of, 70
in the zone, 143
Islam, and demographic swamping,
  89
"I think, therefore I am," 153

jar analogy, 192
Jesus, 72–73
  unrealistic standard of, 91
Jivanmukta, 192
junzi, 140–41
  defined, 45, 87

karma, 167
  belief in, 103
kindness, artificiality of, 87
knowledge, in Confucianism, 54
koans, 169, 173
Krishna, 30, 149–50, 152
Krishnamurti, Jiddu, 124

Lao-tzu, 3. See also Tao Te Ching
  biographical information, 8
  on desires of the eye and the belly,
    136–37
  his art of liberation, 189
  his critique of Confucianism, 103–5
  on impartiality, 128
  on return to the source, 22–25
  as root sage of Taoism, 7–9
  on too many desires, 140
leaving no trace, 154–57
legacies, 156–57
let go and flow, 31–37

li
  defined, 36–37
  discovering, 38–39
  and te, 65
  and ying, 39–41, 144–45
liberation, art of, 187–90
light, 132–33
longevity in Taoism, 68–69
love, unassociated, 177, 187
Loy, David, 166

Malhotra, Rajiv, 94–98, 100
Mao Zedong, 99
martial arts, 3
maya, 24, 111–15
  defined, 111–12
  and qing, 112
McKenna, Terence, 78
measurement, 111–17, 186
  the world beyond, 115–17
meditation
  and letting go of thoughts,
    172–73
  as spiritual solvent, 172–74
Mencius, 106–8
mind
  essence of the, 165
  mind seeking, 169–72
Mitchell, Damo, 100–101
moderation, 38
Moeller, Hans-Georg, 48, 51–53,
    61, 183
monasteries, 151–53
morality, 35, 47
  the amoral reality, 102–8
  Confucian, 47–55
  evil nature of, 88–91
  immorality of, 85–108, 98
  as man-made, 85

produces its opposite, 86–88
  and socialization, 85
  whose is right? 93–102
motion of return, 22–25
Mo-tzu, 110

namarupa, defined, 109
nationalism, separation caused by,
    121–22
natural model, 45–47
naturalness, 31
natural Taoism. See Taoism
nature. See also way of nature
  impartiality of, 109, 130
  regarded as servant of humanity,
    74
  vs. sin, 91–93
  the softness of, 177
  spontaneous natural world, the,
    176–79
Needleman, Jacob, 15–16, 35
Nehru, Jawaharlal, 97
Neidan, defined, 3
Nei Gong, 3
neti neti, 116–17
Nirguna Brahman, and the Tao, 18
nishkam karma, 149–50
nonduality, 101–2
non-dwelling mind, 171
nothingness, bellows metaphor,
    18–19

oneness, 175
  as our house, 161
opposites, universal, 101
original face, 79–84
original nature, 16
ox butchery, 143–46
Ox Mountain story, 106–8

patriotism, 122
Pattanaik, Devdutt, 112
pattern, organic, 35–42
Pink Floyd, 132
Pinyin system, xii
Po-chang, 4
political views, 100–101
pop culture, 78
power aspect of the Tao, 31–32
power corrupts, 52
prajna, 168, 173–74
prajna intuition, 175–76, 192–93
Prakriti, defined, 112–13
Pratyahara, 68
prejudice, 118–20
progress, 100
Purusha, 80

qi, the flow of, 164
qing, 158
    defined, 110
    fasting of, 127

race, as illusion, 119–20
racial communities, 118–20
radical acceptance, 122, 126
radical universalism, 5
    the end of, 97–102
Radio Nonstop Thinking, 151
Ramana Maharshi, 162–63
Ram Swarup, 97
rectification of names philosophy,
    59
regime of sincerity, 48–49
religions
    mutual acceptance of, 93–97
    need for tolerance, 94–97
    separation caused by, 121–22
religious conversion, abolition of, 94

renunciation, 117
resources, consumption of, 75
respect, among religions, 94–98
returning home, 191–93
return to the source, 22–27
    character of the, 25–27
river
    as analogy, 31–35
    of Tao, 184–85
Robber Chih, and Confucius,
    55–60
role playing in Taoism, 60
roles, in Taoism, 60–62
romanization of Chinese words, xii

sage. See Taoist sage
sage's vision, the, 127–31
sainthood, renouncing, 86
salvation, 92
Samsara, 167
samskaras, 167–68
satsang, defined, 152
school, and socialization, 134
Second Noble Truth, 169
security
    inherent, 135–36
    as insecurity, 23
    yearning for, 123
seeing the infinite in all things, 162
seeking, 169–70
self. See also "I"; identity
    illusion of, 166–69
self-cultivation model, 44–45, 139–41
self-esteem, 156–57
    destroyed by socialization, 135
separateness/separation
    as faulty state of mind, 125–26
    four pillars of, 118–22, 176–77
    as fundamental belief, 14, 21–22

sexes
  identifying with sex, 120–21
  inequality of, 120–21
sexual orientation, and sin, 92–93
shadow story, 154–55
Shiva, 24, 113–15
Shiva Lingam with Tripundra, 114–15
  illustration, 114
Shu, 67, 69–71, 73
silence, and abiding in our true
    nature, 163–64
Silicon Valley, influence of, 99
similarities, and differences, 124
simple life, 147–48
simple world
  vs complex world, 132–48
  and simple life, 147
sin, vs. nature, 91–93
sincerity, fake, 48–50
skin color, 118
small picture, and big picture, 16
socialization, 26, 65, 132–37
  and drilling holes in our faces,
    76–79
  as failure, 71
  and isolation, 155
  and longevity, 69
  as a negative indoctrination, 11,
    35, 46, 55, 158
  of our parents, 133–34
  school and, 134
  and seeking, 170
  and this and that, 111
social justice warriors, 98–100
solutions vs. trade-offs, 100
Sowell, Thomas, 100
spiritual master, text as, 144
spontaneous reality, the, 165–79
still-point of the Tao, 19, 72, 161

straw dogs, 128–29
stress, Confucianism and, 50–51
success, 135, 138
suffering
  caused by craving, 169
  and the Taoless reality, 160
Sunyata, 83
superior man, 45, 140–41
Suzuki, Daisetsu Teitaro, 168

t'ai chi, 24, 34–35
  described, 16
  as Tao in motion, 20
  and yin yang, 19–22, 20
T'ai chi t'u, 17
  described, 17–18
Tantra, 92–93
Tao, 65
  attuning to the, 146–48
  as beyond words, 174–75
  defined, 1
  as ever present, 4
  favors no-one, 187
  as immanent and transcendent,
    115–16
  leaving nothing undone, 34
  metaphysical cosmology of the,
    16–22
  nature of the, 30–31
  as nondual oneness, 16
  power aspect of, 31–32
  seeing Tao in all, 162–64
  there is only the, 193
  trying to interfere with the, 93
  as ultimate reality, 15
  white light of, 132–33
Taoism
  accepting it as it is, 10–13
  as attitude, 4

based on texts of Tao Te Ching
and Chuang-tzu, 7
Confucianism critiqued by, 26,
43–62, 86, 103–8
criticisms of, 12–13
defined, 1
as deprogramming, 181
holism and, 3
as immoral, 85, 101–8
must migrate to survive, 9–10
a need for structure in
understanding, 2–5
nonduality and, 101–2, 166
not primitivist, 57
persecution of, 44
as politically incorrect, 101–2
reclaiming, 1–13
and reclaiming health and sanity,
27
role playing in, 60–62
the root of, 7–9
testing it for yourself, 13
three key concepts of, 16–22
as way of nature, 1
Taoist sage. See also sage's vision, the
characteristics of the, 127–31
embodies the Tao, 162
as essence of the universe, 190
failure of, 70–72
and fear, 161
freedom of the, 185–86
has no mission, 188
as perfected state of nature, 127
power of, 129
and prajna intuition, 176
rebellion of the, 60–62
reversed trajectory of the, 16
rules not needed by, 105–6
sage's vision, 127–31

Tao Te Ching, 7, 15–16, 18–20,
30–32, 34, 45–47, 54–55, 68,
86–87, 128, 136, 140–41. See
also Lao-tzu; Taoism
incorrect translations of, 1–2
te
defined, 32
harnessing, 34
and li, 65
ten thousand things, defined, 15–16
text, as spiritual master, 144
thinking
as illusion, 165–69
and illusion of self, 166–69
"this" and "that," 109–11, 116
the birth of, 110–11
thoughts. See also thinking
without language, 174–76
three heavenly principles, 186
tolerance, religious, 94–97
trace, leaving no, 154–57
trade-offs vs. solutions, 100
Traditional Chinese Medicine, 3
translations, 1–2, 6, 8
trident, 114
Tripundra, 114–15
trust, 188
tyrants, 157
Tzu-ch'i, 178
tzu-jan, 163, 165, 174, 180
defined, 31

uncarved block metaphor, 45–47
universe, you as a reflection of the,
14
unlearning, 63–64
unsui, defined, 180
unsupported thought, 166, 168
useless tree story, 177–78

vairagya, defined, 117
vanity, and Confucianism, 52–55
vasanas, 167
Vichara, 172
Vipassana, 172
Vishnu, 24
viveka, defined, 117
Vivekananda, Swami, 93
vrittis, 161

Wade-Giles system, xii
Waidan, defined, 3
Waley, Arthur, 31
wandering, free and easy, 159, 180–93
Wang Pang, 161–62
Warring States period, 42–43
water, as analogy, 25–26
Watson, Burton, 182
Watts, Alan, 27, 36, 53
way of nature, 5, 8, 10, 23, 30, 45–47,
    50, 85. *See also* nature; Taoism
    Taoism as, xi, 1
Wen-hui, Lord, 143
Western culture, 153
wheel and hub description, 19
"When nothing is done nothing is
    left undone," 83, 178
whole, human model of the, 27–31
Wilhelm, Richard, 6, 130–31
wokeism, 98–100
Wong, Eva, 6
worthlessness, and Confucianism,
    51–52
wu chi, 116
    described, 16–19
    as unmanifest aspect of Tao, 18–19

wu-wei, 34, 47, 141
    applying, 9–10
    and becoming nothing, 154–57
    and Cook Ting, 142–43
    deconstructs our framework,
        158
    defined, 9–10, 149–50
    and humility, 177

Xiaogan, Liu, 183
xiaoyao you, 183–84
    defined, 182

yang, defined, 21
Yen Hui, 81–84, 164
yin, defined, 21
ying
    defined, 39–41
    and li, 144–45
yin yang, 28–29
    described, 16–22
    harmony of, 21
    and t'ai chi, 19–22
yoga, defined, 150
you, defined, 182–83
*you*ing, 183
Yugas, 29

zazen, 172
Zen, 80
    and spontaneity, 4
zhen, 61
zhengming, 59
zhenren
    defined, 158–59
    as free and easy wandering, 180